TRANSFORMATIONAL LEADERSHIP

Smyth & Helwys Publishing, Inc.
6316 Peake Road
Macon, Georgia 31210-3960
1-800-747-3016
©2010 by Smyth & Helwys Publishing
All rights reserved.
Printed in the United States of America.

The paper used in this publication meets the minimum requirements of
American National Standard for Information Sciences—
Permanence of Paper for Printed Library Materials.
ANSI Z39.48–1984. (alk. paper)

Library of Congress Cataloging-in-Publication Data

Bugg, Charles B.

Transformational leadership :
leading with integrity / by Charles B. Bugg.
p. cm.
Includes index.
ISBN 978-1-57312-558-1
(pbk. : alk. paper)
1. Christian leadership.
I. Title.
BV652.1.B84 2010
253—dc22
2010016742

TRANSFORMATIONAL
LEADERSHIP

LEADING WITH INTEGRITY

CHARLES B. BUGG

Also by Charles B. Bugg

A Faith to Meet Our Fears: How Your Faith Can Bring Peace, Forgiveness, Wonder…

Lingering Grief: Listening for God in the Pain

Preaching & Intimacy: Preparing the Message and the Messenger

Witness of a Fragile Servant: A Personal Look at Pastoral Preaching

Dedication

To Bob—my younger brother, my friend, and my teacher. Thanks for the example you have set for all of us. Your commitment to Christ, your compassion for others, and your courage to stand up for what matters make you a transformational leader.

Contents

Foreword

I have known Chuck Bugg for many years as a friend and as a superb colleague in the field of homiletics. One of the most impressive things about Chuck is his courageous willingness to venture into new intellectual territory. While deeply grounded in his own theological tradition, Chuck has always hungered to explore new ideas, new methods, and new approaches. In several areas of homiletics—most notably pastoral preaching and creative biblical preaching—he has been eager to put on hiking boots and a backpack and leave the well-established trails in search of fresh wisdom. Running through his creative work, though, is a strong and consistent thread: an emphasis on the personal character of the preacher and church leader.

In this fine volume, the reader can see both characteristics at work—the venturesome spirit and the emphasis on character. Chuck once again pushes himself into new regions of thought, this time in terms of transformational pastoral leadership. His engagement during a sabbatical leave with the ideas of Harvard's Ronald Heifetz and other significant thinkers in the area of leadership, blended with Chuck's own rich store of pastoral wisdom and homiletical insight, has generated a provocative and thoughtful book on the role of the pastoral leader. He shows himself to be profoundly acquainted with the real, on-the-ground challenges and opportunities, conflicts and possibilities, threats and hopes of today's congregations, and he bravely offers his own ministry experience—the failures and fears as well as the triumphs—as an example of how to rethink one's approach to ministry.

Chuck also shows his keen interest in pastoral character. His candid description of the role of leadership in addressing conflict reveals that honest self-assessment is essential to leadership. His detailed analysis of the interpersonal qualities of a leader (chapter 3) is classic Chuck Bugg. In a deeply theological manner, he draws upon the insights of Daniel Goleman, naming the character virtues of a leader: trust, both in the sense of trust in God and faith in other people; the ability of communicating well, that is, a listening spirit that can also speak with conviction and courage; empathy; imagination; and transparency. When I review this list, I am aware of the fact that Chuck is too modest to claim these virtues as his own, but this is precisely the way those who know him would describe him. He is a man of confident faith who is guided by trust in God toward an imaginative engagement with Scripture and an openness and empathy toward others. He is an effective communicator as a preacher, pastor, and teacher. In short, he is exactly the sort of transformational leader this volume intends to encourage.

This would not be a Chuck Bugg book if it did not somewhere take up the ministry of preaching, and he does so in a splendid chapter on the transformational preacher (chapter 5). He summons all who preach to respond to the call to care and to be faithful, even though we are never promised success. Indeed, this urgent need to be faithful even when our faithfulness is not met with what is usually termed "success" is one of the most valuable themes that runs through this book.

Chuck Bugg has not written a book of surefire leadership techniques guaranteed to transform a congregation. He is far too wise for that, and too embedded in the realism of the gospel. Instead, he has written a book that calls all church leaders to embody in their style of interaction with others the qualities of the gospel, which Jesus himself embodied (as Chuck reminds us in chapter 6). Sometimes such leadership takes people toward greater unity, deeper forgiveness, and bolder mission, but even on occasions when good leaders fail, the gospel has been expressed through them nonetheless.

Read these pages, then, with pleasure and for insight, but also with gratitude.

Thomas G. Long
Candler School of Theology
Emory University
Atlanta, Georgia

Preface

I'm tired! It's Sunday night, so I know it's part of the rhythm of my week as a minister. I've spent most of my Sunday nights being tired. However, tonight it's a "good tired." Grace Crossing, the church I serve as intentional interim pastor, has experienced a wonderful weekend.

On Saturday, the folks in the church set up a tent and chairs and provided games and activities for the community. We had bands, and our own worship team provided music. We gave away a free supper (okay, it was hot dogs, chili, slaw, water, and soft drinks, but our church has a limited budget, and we can all eat healthfully the rest of the week).

Among those who attended were people of various ethnic groups and even a young Muslim couple with their two small children. Saturday night as my wife and I talked, we agreed that this is what church should be. "Red, yellow, black, and white, they are precious in his sight." I grew up singing that song but not always seeing its reality in churches I attended. It was a beautiful sight to see that song lived out in a field where one day the people of Grace Crossing hope to build a church. Maybe, in ways we didn't even realize, we were already building a church.

On Sunday morning, we worshiped under the tent, and I could see the looks on the people's faces. Perhaps it's because I was writing a book on transformational leadership that I saw something else. I saw leadership. I watched people assuming responsibilities, taking initiative toward strangers and making them welcome, being compassionate with each other, and doing everything they could to reflect the presence of God.

Sharon Daloz Parks wrote *Leadership Can Be Taught*.[1] Parks makes the case that we all can be more effective leaders if we do our parts to make the world a better place. Leaders are not simply born with charisma and charm. Leaders are those who want to do whatever they can to make their corners of the world more loving places. Some people have God-given gifts to stand in front of a group and articulate a bold vision with passion and power. Other folks have God-given gifts to encourage, to love, and to make people feel more at home. These are also leaders, whether they would call themselves that or not.

I'm grateful to people in churches and in institutions who have endured my limitations and encouraged me in my successes. I thank my own cloud of witnesses for love and care. I couldn't possibly have done anything without the love of my family. If anybody knows my failings, it's my family, and yet they have never ceased to love me. Diane, my wife, has stood beside me in the thick and thin of life and taught me more than any other human being the meaning of unconditional love.

When I began the Center for Transformational Leadership at Gardner-Webb University in 2007, I met Susan Jenkins. The provost said, "She will be your assistant." Susan hardly needed more work because she was already the administrative assistant for the university's nursing school. Dr. Susie Beck-Little, the dean of the nursing school, was gracious to share Susan with me. I've now spent enough time in the nursing school that I believe I deserve a pin and my own stethoscope. Susan became more than an assistant. When the Honorable Max Cleland, former senator from Georgia, spoke on our campus, Susan made certain that all the details were in place. She also helped me take my words off of notepads and put them into the right form for the publisher. I could not have asked for a better assistant and friend.

As you read this book, you can quickly tell that much of my ministry has involved preaching or teaching preaching. At times, the homiletical emphasis probably trumps the leadership focus. Yet, in writing this book, I found that I couldn't neglect my love for preaching and how strongly it is connected to my view of leadership.

Note

1. Sharon Daloz Parks, *Leadership Can Be Taught: A Bold Approach for a Complex World* (Boston: Harvard Business School Press, 2005).

Introduction

In fall 2004, I had the opportunity to do a sabbatical leave at the John F. Kennedy School of Government at Harvard University. Dr. Ronald Heifetz was my mentor. I sat in his class and marveled at his insights.

I also marveled at what was truly a "Renaissance person." If Heifetz's skill and understanding of what he termed "adaptive leadership" weren't enough to impress me, he was also a graduate of Harvard University's medical school with specialization in psychiatry *and* a world-class cellist. Frankly, I was not only impressed but also intimidated. Those of us who have at most "one talent" and sometimes question the level of that talent are easily overwhelmed by people like Heifetz who seem to have it all.

Despite my fears, I found my time with Ron Heifetz extremely rewarding. I learned and was challenged to think about leadership in ways I never anticipated.

I deliberately chose a "secular" environment in which to study. It's not that I reject the Bible or my Christian faith as being deficient, but I wanted to hear what people other than clergy or religiously oriented folks said about the issues of leadership. In fact, I was the only minister in the class. Surrounded by people whose varied backgrounds and worldviews differed from mine, I was pleasantly reminded not only of diversity in our world but also our shared intentions as leaders and members of the human family.

Ron Heifetz is a devout Jew and appropriately inserted his faith perspective into portions of the class. When I made arrangements to study with him, I knew little about him other than what I read in some of his writings and what I learned from the recommendations of respected friends who had heard him speak.

Frankly, I expected I would have to "baptize" almost everything I heard. I have spent my vocational life in churches and in institutions that affirm the Christian faith. I anticipated that I would hear excellent information about leadership and then need to convert it to my faith tradition. In fact, as a Baptist, I would probably need to find verses in the Bible and drag them out, "kicking and screaming," as support for what I said.

The fact is that, surprisingly, the distance between what Heifetz said in the hallowed halls of Harvard and what I say in the sanctuary of a church or an institution where I teach is not so great. When Heifetz talked about a leader's having a "sacred heart" and that the purpose of a leader was to draw out the good in people, I felt at home. Maybe I didn't have a biblical text right at hand, but I certainly heard concepts that seemed consistent with what I believed.

More than just teaching me ideas, however, my experience at the Kennedy School renewed my passion to understand more about leadership. Not only did I want to be a more effective leader myself, but also I wanted to help students, clergy colleagues, and people in churches better understand what it means to lead.

Does this mean I am an expert on leadership? Hardly! In fact, I'm convinced that the more we study something, the more the territory for learning grows and the more we find to explore. At least that is true for an area like leadership where there are a variety of opinions about what constitutes effective leadership. Some folks contend that leaders are born, not made, so they wonder what's the use of trying to teach a subject for which some people have no capacity.

Obviously, I don't agree with people who argue that leaders are born, not made. We are all genetically predisposed in some ways, and we are partially formed by the ways in which we are nurtured or not nurtured. These things help shape us and undoubtedly influence our capacity to develop in certain areas.

For example, my son-in-law is an astrophysicist. Some believe that daughters marry husbands who somehow resemble their fathers, but our family counters that theory. In college, I took the minimal math and science courses. Then I headed for the English and Social Science areas where things made more sense and I felt academically "at home."

Could I have been an astrophysicist if I had tried? I doubt it. But I could have taken more math and science courses and probably been better for it. At least, it would have given me a platform on which to stand and at least have a semi-intelligent conversation with Bryan, our son-in-law. As it is, we usually talk about sports and family, or I listen as he speaks about black holes, new galaxies, and a variety of other fascinating subjects.

Each of us can be a better leader. We may never occupy a formal place of leadership or even be labeled by others as a leader, but we may influence somebody to do the right thing or serve as the voice in the group that calls members to focus on important items. In doing that, we may show more leadership than the president of an organization who never takes necessary risks, who fails to communicate with the people in the institution, and who has little idea about how to help people focus on a mission.

I address this book to those of us who are a part of the Christian faith and who try to exercise leadership in the church or a Christian institution or organization. If this book falls into the hands of somebody outside my perspective, I hope and even pray that what I say is helpful.

Chapter 1

A Description of Transformational Leadership

I grew up trying to define the terms. In 1960 and 1961, Roger Fendrick and I traveled the state of Florida debating the subject "Resolved that the United Nations Should Be Significantly Strengthened." Our debate coach, Miss McClure, would have subscribed to the legendary football coach Vince Lombardi's admonition, "Winning isn't the main thing; it's the only thing!"

With finger wagging and eyes staring through us, Miss McClure inveighed, "Define your terms! Make the opposing team play on your field." Roger and I took her advice to heart. Our words became our swords. We seized on the word "significantly." If we debated on the "negative side," we would attack our opponent's plan as not being significant enough. "Significantly" is not well defined. What is significant? Our strategy was that either something was not significant or, if it seemed significant, the United Nations didn't have the will or the mechanisms to implement it.

With the passing of time, I'm less into defining and more into describing. Miss McClure would not approve, but now I don't need her approval. Besides, description is more compatible with the poetic, narrative style that characterizes the pedagogy of many disciplines.

Leadership is a combination of art and science. To say that another way, effective leaders are people who are always studying their strengths and weaknesses and examining the skills and strategies that can make them better in what they do.

In describing transformational leadership, I want to give attention to the word "transformational." What does it mean to be engaged in the process of transformation?

Transformation as Process

We need to recognize that transformation is a process. It is a process of change and hopefully growth as compassionate and competent human beings. Measuring growth in competency is easier than measuring growth in areas like compassion. Many of us who teach classes conduct a pre-test and a post-test. The pre-test measures the level of knowledge that a student possesses coming into a course. The post-test, hopefully, indicates that this student has learned something during the semester.

However, some important qualities are difficult to measure quantifiably. How do we measure somebody's growth in awareness of other people's concerns and her empathy with people's needs? We think we know these things when we see them, but they are qualities of life that transcend precise measurement.

The fact is that some of the most important components of life cannot be quantified. Recently, a dear woman wrote me a beautiful letter about her long marriage. "I love him more now than the day I said, 'I do.'" I have no reason to doubt her. Since I know the couple well, I have watched their relationship move through the changing seasons of life. I wouldn't doubt that her love for her spouse has developed and matured. Love, however, is not something that we can put in a mathematical formula to prove that there is more love today than yesterday.

Yet, abandoning qualities like faith, hope, and love just because we can't measure them precisely is forsaking what makes life worth living. With leadership, we learn some ideas that can be measured by their implementation, but we also encounter qualities out of which we choose to live that transcend human measurement.

Later in the book, I want to talk about specific attributes of a transformational leader. Here, I will linger on the word "transformational" and describe what I see as its essence.

The Belief that You and I Can Change

People often say to each other, "Just be yourself." Who can argue with authenticity and integrity? After all, each of us is largely a product of our genetic makeup, life experiences, opportunities or lack of opportunities, and countless other factors. When somebody tells us to be ourselves, that person may simply be saying to us, "You are what you are, and that's okay."

However, the call to be ourselves is sometimes an excuse not to make needed changes. Most of us develop some self-defeating and self-destructive behaviors. We may recognize aspects of ourselves that we need to change, but we say, "This is who I am. I can't change, and I won't change!" Our unwillingness to change or become different prevents us from developing life skills and attitudes that help us function as caring and compassionate members of larger communities.

For example, many people who occupy formal positions of leadership have a strong sense of "ego." In one way, that's good. We want our leaders to be confident, decisive, and unafraid to take appropriate risks. But what if that ego causes an individual to believe that she is always right and never needs to seek the counsel of others, creating an environment in which her colleagues and employees are afraid to question any of her decisions.

The same ego or self-esteem may cause a person to be perceived as a decisive leader, but also as a leader who is not open to the insights and opinions of others. What masquerades as strength is sometimes actually fear of being questioned or a need to receive credit for every good thing that happens. This type of person is also quick to shift responsibility to someone else when something does not go well. People in leadership who operate this way are frequently referred to as those who "throw somebody else under the bus." This form of scapegoating is a manifestation of low self-esteem. No one is always successful, and while seeking the input of others, we need to acknowledge when we make a mistake.

Those of us who are Christians often speak about the grace of God. We talk about grace, but we often find it difficult to appropriate in our lives. Grace is "God's unmerited favor," but what does that look like? As a person or as a leader, how does grace affect the way I see myself and the ways in which I interact with others?

For instance, am I able to acknowledge my personal limits and need for growth? Pride is frequently the most serious impediment to any kind of personal growth. Believing I must do everything perfectly or blaming others for anything that goes wrong keeps me from examining my heart and the ways in which I deal with people. Theologically, I'm denying that I am accepted and loved even when I fail.

In terms of a church or institution, the leader who is unable or unwilling to admit mistakes creates an atmosphere in which people are less inclined to be creative and take risks. If the leader of a group attempts to find someone who will be the scapegoat for a failure, then people will not think "outside the box"; instead, they will simply do things as they have always done them. Taking risks creates the potential for failure, and many people don't want to risk failing and then taking the blame for it.

For ministers or other leaders who work with church staffs or other people whom they supervise, this is particularly important to remember. Staff relations can become problematic for churches and institutions. As churches, we affirm that all ministers are called by God, not hired by the church. While almost everyone agrees that this is true theologically, the difficulty comes in the practical implications of people called by God working together for a common purpose.

In many churches, confusion abounds around the issue of authority. Who has the authority to make decisions regarding the ministers of the church? What if a minister is underperforming? Is there any accountability? To whom is that minister responsible? Are there structures in place to deal with persons who try to create their own constituencies and power bases?

I could cite countless other examples. What about the autocratic pastor who has to have everything his way? What about the minister who never accepts responsibility for her mistakes and who always finds something or someone to blame? In the worst-case scenario, how do we deal with a church staff that has lost respect for each other, where any vestige of teamwork has vanished, where backbiting and blaming are the primary ways of interaction, and where distrust is the operative word?

Can this kind of dysfunctional system change? Can individuals who are not functioning effectively and who have adopted self-serving tactics to camouflage their ineffectiveness learn to become part of the team and pull their weight as individual ministers?

The answer is a qualified yes. People can change. That is a fundamental part of our Christian faith. No one is beyond God's capacity to make us different. However, this is where the "yes" is qualified.

During my ministry, I have been amazed at several unfortunate ways in which churches often deal with staff problems or the performance of individual ministers. First, some things are tolerated that church members' companies or businesses would never accept. While no church is like IBM or Bank of America, the fact is that the church has the most important mission in the world. We don't want the church to adopt the business model for the body of Christ, but we have every reason to expect ministers to see their callings as supremely important.

If there are emotional, family, or other reasons that a person cannot fulfill his responsibilities, the church can deal with the individual redemptively. Hopefully, the leaders of the church understand the needs of ministers and the fact that ministers deal with the same burdens, challenges, and difficulties that all human beings face. In fact, ministers' struggles are often exacerbated by other people's expectations of them, or even by their expectations of themselves or their families.

The Difficulty of Change

While Christians affirm that God's grace can change who we are and the way we live, change is difficult. Change is difficult both for individuals and for institutions.

To use the image of a church and its staff members, how does change happen, if it happens? We can avoid change by thinking that things will work out if we simply hope and pray enough. Obviously, the power of prayer is critical. However, prayer is sometimes used as an excuse not to do something uncomfortable. As Jesus reminded us, "Is there anyone among you who, if your child asks for bread, will give a stone? Or if the child asks for a fish, will give a snake?" (Matt 7:9-10, NRSV)

Prayer precedes action on our parts. It doesn't replace the need for action. Hopefully, we act in the spirit of prayer. However, as a wise minister reminded me, "There is no painless way to do painful things." Even when we try to do something with kindness and care for the people concerned, there is no way to avoid some pain.

Nobody wants to be part of a church or an institution where people are treated as objects and no concern is shown for the hurt inflicted on persons and their families. At the same time, no church or institution wants to move to the other side where underperformance is tolerated because the church says, "As Christians, we should not do anything that is unkind."

The result is often toleration of ministers or employees whose lack of initiative or inability to perform their jobs causes the whole group to fall short of its mission. Is it Christian for a minister to shirk his responsibilities and then hide under the cover of his calling? "I'm called by God to this church," he might say, "and no one should call me to task."

On the other hand, let's remember that there are people in any organization who expect too much and criticize constantly. A healthy church knows how to keep these types of personalities from moving to places of leadership where their own neuroses complicate the situation. Sadly, some churches allow such people to "bully" or "intimidate" their way into positions of authority. The unwillingness to confront appropriately these types of so-called leaders creates "dis-ease" that affects the morale of the church staff as well as the entire congregation.

Change is possible, but most change is hard. It begins with an honest assessment of who we are and an acknowledgment of our strengths and weaknesses. People who work in the area of "emotional intelligence" tell us that effective leaders not only possess the intellectual intelligence to think through problems but also the emotional intelligence to understand themselves and others. That means good leaders recognize who they are and know their personal assets and limits. These same leaders are empathetic with others and realize the cost of change.

For those of us in ministry, recognizing our limits is difficult. When we seek a position and interview with representatives from a particular church, we understand quickly that the church's expectations for their ministers are usually unrealistic. Our temptation is to tell these committees that we can do all that they ask and do all of it well. Of course, we set ourselves up for failure.

Churches Need to Change

Part of the transformation must begin with the church itself. Since I now serve a number of interim pastorates, I'm always fascinated by the job descriptions pastor search committees develop. Most of these descriptions begin with a survey of the church members. The members are asked to indicate their priorities in what they want in a pastor. Then the committee calculates the results, and a list of expectations for the new pastor emerges.

Frequently, the list of expectations is too lengthy and involves a combination of skills and gifts that few, if any, potential ministers possess. Certain qualities may be listed as more important. For example, the ability to preach and teach is at the top of most churches' wish lists. However, churches list a dozen other things as important to them. The fact is that while visiting the home-bound, for example, is not at the top of the list for the whole church, it is at the top of the list for those whose family members are no longer able to attend church.

Leaders in the church must be more realistic and communicate that realism to the congregation before the church begins searching for a new minister. People in a church need to understand that there is no way a minister can meet each person's expectations, and the members need to deal with this reality before considering someone for a call. Too often, a church avoids this crucial work, and the result is a frustrated congregation with a discouraged minister.

Part of the church's motivation is not just practical but also biblical. Read the book of Acts, and you won't get far before you find the Apostles asking for help. The Apostles are not able to give attention to the study of the word, and so they ask for "diakonos" to help them minister to the widows.

Of course, some people are quick to point out that now we pay the preacher to do the work. After all, some folks volunteer their time. In the first century, the Apostles didn't receive a salary with benefits.

All of that may be true, but carried to its illogical conclusion, it creates a twisted ecclesiology. Trained clergy become the players, and laypersons become the spectators. As long as the game goes well, the paying and non-paying customers are content. However, spectators are quick to change their opinions when the "professionals" are not performing up to their expectations. This view of the church is a set-up for an "us against them" mentality.

What can we do to create a healthful view of the church that sees clergy and laypersons as colleagues and not adversaries in achieving a mission? Perhaps we can begin with a sensible ecclesiology. Times have changed between the first century and the twenty-first century. Many churches have professional clergy. Some of these ministers have attended seminary and divinity school.

Ministers are trained to do certain things. Any church should expect particular competencies from a minister. However, saying that a minister is trained to do everything well and is called by the church to be the resident expert on every aspect of ministry, theology, pastoral care, and the business affairs of the church is setting the bar way too high. Disappointment results for everyone.

Instead of a church adopting a "spectator" or even an "adversarial" role toward the pastor, what if it chose the "collaborative" model? This assumes that clergy are called to do ministry *with* people and not just *for* people. The Apostle Paul's striking image of the church as a body is a collaborative image. A healthy body is one in which all the parts function in cooperation with each other. The body operates in response to impulses from the brain or the head. Again, Paul underscores that the church belongs to Christ and functions in response to Christ's purposes for the body.

Ministers Need to Change

Leadership does not mean that any of us does everything right or that we must be successful in each aspect of our work. Leadership not only demands risk, but it also requires a willingness to learn from mistakes and to forgive ourselves for being humans who sometimes fail God, ourselves, and others.

One of the great barriers to change is pride. While most of us in ministry like to imagine ourselves as humble servants, an insidious pride may keep us from the personal growth that comes from recognizing both our strengths and weaknesses. Part of this stems from the nature of our vocation. While many churches affirm the community of believers and the fact that each believer is called to ministry, there is something special about those who are called to the clergy.

In the Baptist church where I grew up, the pastor referred to this call as "full-time Christian service." At the end of each service, our pastor issued an "invitation." People were invited to come to the front of the sanctuary to share decisions with the church body. My home church was especially pleased when one of the young people felt "called" to "full-time Christian service." The church felt affirmed in its ministry of nurture, and the congregation warmly embraced the person. In some ways, a commitment like this assured the future of the church. Also, it indicated that a church was doing a good job encouraging young people to consider a vocation of Christian service.

What happened, however, in my own mind was the confusion of my calling and identity. Whether I heard this from others in the church or whether I arrived at the conclusion myself, this idea that I had to embody the virtues of being a minister became problematic. The main problem was the idea that I had to have the answers or that I had to pretend I had them. Perhaps this is endemic to any profession in which people tend to look to the person for guidance or help.

However, for me the issue was that I perceived my calling and my personal identity as one and the same. I felt the pressure to be an example in the way I lived and the decisions I made. You can imagine the difficulty with all the normal tensions of adolescence and the self-imposed stress to think and act in ways that I thought others expected and that I expected of myself.

I suppose there is nothing wrong with trying to be an example to others unless we take ourselves too seriously. Taking ourselves too seriously leads to a kind of isolationism that keeps us from hearing both the positive and negative things and the full range of feedback that is essential to leadership. Isolation keeps us from the type of transparency and openness that allow other folks to enter our lives with their gifts of grace, as well as their caring words about how we can be more effective ministers.

Some people refer to this process as "closing the loop" or "360-degree feedback." Effective leaders develop ways to encourage people in their groups to feel free to offer suggestions and to develop processes by which to give that input. Secure leaders don't see this as a threat but rather as a way to help people feel "ownership" in the church or institution and to secure the wider feedback that is vital to effective leadership.

The idea that a minister or leader of a group must generate all the ideas or that we have to be correct in every decision will result in increasing isolation of ourselves. Also, it will kill the creative spirit of any organization and ultimately may result in the group's sabotaging of what the leader wants.

Ownership of ideas is important in the healthy functioning of any institution. Leaders who need credit for every positive idea may unwittingly create people in the organization who may sabotage the implementation of those ideas because they feel that they never played a significant part in the development of the goals and strategies. Leaders may wrongly interpret a vote for something as a personal commitment by the members of the group that they will give their full support to the implementation of the plan.

Thus, potential leaders need to examine how important it is for them to achieve their personal agendas. If achieving our objectives means we are inattentive to the opinions of people with whom we work, then we need to work at paying attention to what people say. What we try to achieve is a collaborative working style. That doesn't mean any of us surrenders our dreams if someone has concerns or objections, but it does mean we understand that in order to achieve big dreams, the must be supportive. Some of us who like to do everything before sundown must work to be patient and try to gain support for what we want to achieve. If we don't have the "buy-in" at the beginning, we usually find that we carry the project by ourselves.

Changing from the Inside Out

Transformational leadership involves acquiring the skills and knowledge to help effect positive change in the world around us. But what about the world within each of us? What keeps us from being secure enough with ourselves to take the risks that are demanded in leaders? Why do we affirm the importance of compassion and empathy and then find our lives wound tightly around ourselves and our ambitions? In a word, how do we attempt to be transformative when we resist the changes that make us better people?

Transformational leadership involves a deep look within ourselves to ask the question that Soren Kierkegaard posed: "How can we be a Christian when we are already one of sorts?" Kierkegaard was concerned that we actualize in the way we live those things, such as compassion and care, that we profess to believe. Transformation is a continuous process. It forces those of us who want to lead others to examine ourselves and constantly ask, "In what ways do we need to allow God to change us to make us more compassionate, caring people?"

To utilize the language of "emotional intelligence," how do we become more self-aware and then manage ourselves so that we can be the caring leaders that God calls us to be? This is not a journey for the faint of heart or for those who believe leadership is merely learning a set of skills. Transformational leadership is the call to a journey in which we God continuously changes us and in which we call others to make a positive difference in the world.[1]

Note

1. John Ryan, President and CEO of the Center for Creative Leadership, writes about "6 Keys to Leading in Turbulent Times." The first key to effective leadership is "collaboration." Ryan observes, "Collaborative leaders can get tremendous results. CCL research shows that the ability to collaborate is a skill that top executives believe their men and women should have. In fact, 97 percent of the executives we surveyed identified collaboration as a key to their organization's success. And yet, just 47 percent of those same executives believe the leaders in their organizations are skilled collaborators." (Center for Creative Leadership, e-newsletter, October 2008, p. 1)

Chapter 2

Personal Qualities of a Transformational Leader

One way to examine transformational leadership is to look at personal qualities a leader embodies and reflects in his or her work with people. This involves more than just the way a leader treats people. Rather, these qualities are part of a transformational leader's character. One cannot take them off and put them on like a dress or a suit of clothes; instead, they are an integral part of the basic values a leader holds. While no person has perfected these qualities, they seem imperative to effective leadership. Leaders should work to develop these qualities.

The following four qualities—trust, passion, humility, and coherence—and their significant components are essential in a strong leader.

Trust

Can we trust a particular leader to seek the best for other people? Or is the leader so concerned about her own ambitions and needs that she sees the people she leads as serving her? Being a trustworthy leader requires commitment, consistency, competence, and compassion.

Commitment

A leader is committed to the mission of the institution he serves. If the leader is a pastor of a church, this means he is committed to the purpose of the church—broadly defined as making known the good news of the God revealed through Jesus Christ. Within that broad definition, a church may describe itself in terms of the fundamental strategies the congregation uses to accomplish its mission. For example, some churches see their primary task as evangelism, bringing new people to faith in Jesus Christ. Other congregations stress social justice, that is, helping the oppressed, the marginalized, and the neglected to know of God's care for them.

A leader must remember the mission to which the church is called. A congregation does not exist to meet a minister's needs. A church is not the place for a minister to further her own agenda, agree with all of her requests, or become the means through which personal ambitions are achieved.

The church needs to trust that its minister has its mission as his fundamental priority and is called with the members to try to accomplish that mission. Does that mean everybody in the church agrees on the purpose? Of course not! In almost every congregation, certain people want to shape the church in their images and are not above using devious means to accomplish this.

However, if a pastor begins to act in the same self-serving way, then the true ministry of the church is lost. Sacrificing our integrity in order to try to "defeat" others is the way to win a battle, but, sadly, we lose the war for our own souls. A leader keeps his focus on the mission of the institution and calls people to share that focus. Doing so does not guarantee success, but it ensures that we can look in the mirror and recognize the minister God has called us to be.

Consistency

Another important factor in gaining trust is the consistency with which a leader treats people. How do we perceive those with whom we work? Naturally, each of us is attracted to certain types of people. Usually, those people are most like us and give us the feedback we want.

On the other hand, there are some with whom we must work hard to establish any kind of relationship. Even that relationship may involve minimum conversation. Some people are intimidated by the fact that we are ministers. They realize that we are usually educated, and they assume that we know far more about the Bible than they do (little do they know how much we don't know).

Some people have little or no response to our ministry. We may falsely conclude that they don't like or appreciate us. What we don't recognize is that some people to whom we minister don't know how to express verbal gratitude. They are like the uncle at a family Christmas gathering who responds to your gift with something like, "I really don't need this," or "You shouldn't have." You wish he'd just take the bundle of socks and say, "Thank you."

Other people resist our ideas, and we may exclude them from those who agree with us. We connect only with those who give us favorable reviews and nod their heads affirmatively at our every notion. Unfortunately, this deprives us of the benefit of balanced counsel, and it also creates an environment of perceived favoritism. Certain people have access to the leaders, while others feel that their voices are never heard.

Inconsistency in the way a leader treats people is not only antithetical to the biblical perspective that all people are important as God's children, but is also detrimental to the work of the group. It causes division within the group and stifles the creativity and energy of folks who feel disregarded. For any program to have sustained support, the leader must have the strong backing of the people with whom he works. Otherwise, people may acquiesce to what the leader wants but sabotage it by not following through on their work or by exhibiting other passive-aggressive behaviors.

Competence

Obviously, people are more inclined to cooperate with a leader they perceive as competent. Competence does not mean the leader has all the answers, but that the people in the organization believe the leader is focused on the mission and has a sense of direction. For example, the pastor of a church needs to know something of who he is and what he's supposed to do. A certain level of competence is expected. You don't want to begin your ministry by saying, "Now, what am I supposed to do, and how am I expected to do it?"

As a minister, I have watched churches develop their expectations for a pastor. I've noted the pivotal place of preaching in what most congregations value in their pastors. Without exception, every church I have served as pastor or interim pastor has said that they want effective proclamation. People define effectiveness differently, but usually they mean they want somebody who combines substance with an attractive delivery. People seem hungry for a word from Scripture that connects with the needs in their lives. Churches also want to know what their mission is and how they can move outside of their walls to be the missional people of God.

However, preaching does other things that are integrally related to the function of a pastor as leader. According to the minister's preparation or lack of study, his command of the pulpit, and his confidence or lack of confidence, those who listen will make judgments about the competency of their ministers.

Several years ago when I was on vacation, I went to hear a friend preach. While the sermon itself was fine, several things that happened during the worship service made me question how seriously he took this hour of worship that is so critical to many people's lives. For one thing, he, the choir, and the rest of the worship leaders entered five minutes late. I'm aware that not everybody is as compulsive about time as I am. When the service began, no one offered a reason for the delay. I noticed that when the staff took their seats in the front, most of them slumped in their chairs, looking distracted, and generally gave the impression that this was the last place they wanted to be.

Again, I'm aware of my predilections about the way people approach worship. I don't like the stilted, overly formal way that some ministers handle a service. Authenticity sails out the sanctuary window when people give contrived inflections to words like "God" or emphasis the first syllable of "*Je*sus." Neither is anything gained by a ministerial staff that sits uncomfortably straight or wears plastic smiles.

However, being late and slumping in chairs is not the answer. We come to the event of worship with the sense that God is there to meet us; that we have done our best to prepare; and that we have something important to offer to God and to the church.

All of this is to say that the competence of a leader is measured not only by what he knows but also by the way he presents himself. A leader needs to be aware of both the importance of the message and the ways in which to motivate people most effectively to achieve the goals of the organization. Knowing these things helps create the confidence a leader needs. Then the leader can work to avoid personal idiosyncrasies such as slouching in the chair, tapping on a table with fingers, or interrupting others in the group.

Compassion

To gain the trust of people with whom we work, we need to show them compassion. Each person in a congregation is different. Some of them have been formed by experiences of life that shape them in ways that make it difficult for us to understand them and sometimes even to tolerate them.

Exhibiting compassion is much like expressing empathy. As best we can, we try to understand what makes each of us behave and respond in certain ways. Rather than expecting everybody to see and do life the way we do, we try to listen to people as individuals. We listen not only to the words but also to the passion, sensitivity, intonation, affect, or lack of feeling in what is said. Often, we reveal more about ourselves by how we say something than simply by what we say.

When I was taking a unit of Clinical Pastoral Education, my supervisor pointed out to me a pattern that I sometimes used to avoid engagement with the group. My supervisor said I tried to co-lead the group with him, and he didn't need a co-leader. What I needed was involvement with the members of my interpersonal group.

I spoke in a monotonal, measured way, pulling myself out of the give and take of the group by making observations about other people's issues. What I didn't do was talk about my fears, my concerns, or the things or people that had shaped and in some ways misshaped me. My supervisor heard the music beneath my monotone, and he sensed that all was not as harmonious as I pretended. His confrontation was an act of compassion that invited me to open those shadowy places of myself that needed to be exposed and explored.

Having compassion as a leader does not mean we allow people to run over us or manipulate us. However, as leaders, we recognize the types of people who cause us to overreact, and we are able to keep our focus and balance when somebody seeks to subvert our leadership by intimidation or personal attack. Compassion allows us to care even for those whom we perceive to be our enemies because leadership is not about defeating somebody but achieving a needed result.

Passion

Trustworthiness is an essential quality of a leader. Passion is also imperative. While the word "passion" has many nuances, I mean being committed to a truly worthwhile cause. If our cause is only our own success, then we become self-centered and self-serving. It is far better to be committed and passionate about something that will help other people and make our world a better place.

In the letter to the Philippians, we find these wonderful words: "Finally, beloved, whatever is true, whatever is honorable, whatever is just, whatever is pure, whatever is pleasing, whatever is commendable, if there is any excellence and if there is anything worthy of praise, think about these things" (Phil 4:8 NRSV). In the deepest sense, this is a call to move outside ourselves and focus on what is truly essential.

We often lose focus when we allow someone else to distract us from the important things. Ministers encounter opposition. Not everyone agrees with everything I want to do. Not everyone thinks I am as good a minister as the people in my home church used to tell me I was.

What does opposition or conflict do to us? Warren Bennis, the respected leadership guru, speaks about a leader being taken out of his game. We are taken out of the game when our desire to please or our pain at the idea that somebody may oppose our plans becomes the center of our thinking. We focus on winning and defeating someone else in the process, or we abandon our dreams and recede into irrelevancy.

Interestingly, the affirmation of others can blur our focus and make us believe that we are oblivious to failure. Things or people seduce us away so that we forget what we are called to be and to do, and who calls us. While many in ministry think too little of their gifts, some think too highly of themselves and fail to remember that given a set of circumstances, none of us is incapable of sabotaging our ministries by believing that we don't have to play by the moral and ethical rules that we teach others.

When I was a seminary student, a wise teacher reminded me that there was nothing I couldn't do given the pressures that I would face as a minister. I was surprised because I viewed myself as a moral, ethical person with a strong sense of integrity. My professor was talking about times when we felt badly about ourselves, when people criticized us, and when we lost focus and passion for what we did.

We look for something or someone to make us feel better about ourselves, often with the result of doing something that sabotages our ministries. The most obvious example is the minister who has a sexual affair. Several of the most gifted ministers I know have hurt their ministries and especially the people who look to them as examples by having affairs. The Internet has added another dimension with the copying of sermons that are then preached as the minister's own work or even the downloading of sexually explicit material. It is easy to stand at a distance and pass judgment on these behaviors. Our Christian faith calls us to fidelity in relationships and honesty in our work.

Yet, we need to ask more questions about why these things happen. All of us who are ministers are flawed and vulnerable in different ways. The pressures we face may cause us to respond in ways that reflect those vulnerabilities. We forget our primary passion to serve and to glorify God. We look for something to make us feel better at least temporarily, but in the process we sacrifice the vocation, the call, that God has given us.

None of us is naïve enough to say that staying focused on our calling to follow God will eliminate the problems that tempt us to lose that focus. Frankly, we need to acknowledge that ministers never stop being human beings. People who are manipulative, predatory, and abuse the power that comes with the calling are in positions of ministry. This is simply an acknowledgment that ministers are humans and remain human long after the ordination certificate is signed and hanging on the walls of our offices.

Passion as a Result of Spiritual Disciplines

While the word "passion" may suggest a feeling, it is more an act of discipline or response to God. The death of Jesus is often referred to as his Passion. The root of the word "passion" is the same as the root for words like "passive." In the death of Jesus, our Lord was being "acted upon." In effect, Jesus surrendered his own volition in order to follow God's purpose. In Jesus' prayer in the garden of Gethsemane, he voiced this surrender to the Divine purpose: "not my will but thine be done."

Therefore, passion is not built on continuous excitement or enjoyment of what we do. In fact, we all have times when we don't "feel" like doing what we have to do. Plus, not everything is particularly meaningful or pleasurable to us as ministers. I have sat in committee meetings wondering about all the other things I had to do, thinking, "Why didn't anyone ever tell me there would be moments like this in the ministry?"

This is where personal spiritual disciplines such as prayer, Sabbath, and Bible reading can keep us focused. In those times, God acts on us to remind us that we are dependent on the grace and mercy of God. Passion is not something that we will for ourselves, but it results from the surrender of who we are to the Holy One.

Humility

In a world that prizes personal ambition and self-promotion, humility is often misconstrued. Humble people are thought to be those with no backbone or confidence who are generally pushed around by more assertive individuals.

That is a profound misunderstanding. From the Latin word *humus*, which is usually translated "earthy," a humble person is one who knows her own earthiness and who does not have to pretend that she possesses power and perceptions that belong only to God. A humble leader is actually more confident because he doesn't have to act as if he knows all the answers or take credit for the accomplishments of an institution of which he is a part. The ability of a leader to take appropriate blame and allow others to share in the credit is essential to the functioning of a healthy group. Affirming others and giving credit for good work are signs of self-confidence. In fact, a leader who wants all the credit and none of the blame displays a lack of what the proponents of emotional quotient call self-awareness and social awareness.

If we are aware of ourselves, we recognize that we don't function in isolation. We depend on others to extend the message of the Christ. It is not all about us. We are interdependent and remember what the Apostle Paul affirmed: "We are all part of the body, and none of us is the whole body" (Eph 5:31-3).

Leaders learn to share both the praise and the blame. People work harder and with more creativity in an environment of support and encouragement. Praise needs to be genuine, rising from a heart secure in its relationship with God and grateful for those who share the work of ministry with us.

Coherence

For my birthday, my daughter gave me a book titled *Leading Coherently: Reflections from Leaders around the World*.[1] A fascinating compilation of essays from a variety of leaders across the globe, this book asks not only what *calls* a person to be a leader but also what *sustains* that leader.

A key to sustaining leadership is coherence. Coherence begins with a journey inside ourselves to see what is crucial to us and what holds us together as a person during times of crisis. Then, coherence extends outward as we attempt to keep other people aware of what can sustain them, especially in times of turmoil.

Being a Coherent Person

While the word "coherence" does not appear in the Bible, the concepts of wholeness and focus on what is ultimately important fill the pages of both the Hebrew Bible and the New Testament. In times when the people of God were overwhelmed, God did not call them to forget their pain but rather to remember the sufficiency and strength of the Holy One. God calls us to focus our faith on the unchanging mercy, love and loving-kindness of God.

People who are called to positions of leadership do not stop being people. As persons, we confront unexpected changes in our lives, disappointments, heartaches, grief, and all the other facets of living that people face. Henri Nouwen, the Roman Catholic priest and noted spiritual guide, captured the attention of many in a book called *The Wounded Healer*. Using this powerful image, Nouwen described the minister as one who is called to tend to other people's wounds while at the same caring for his own wounds.[2]

This was a liberating word for many of us in ministry. Some of us believed that we had to minister to others from pedestals. We knew we were human, but we found it hard to confess our own anger, anguish, and despair. Those of us with families faced the issues that arise in the context of intimate relationships, but we believed we had to assume a public "persona" and pretend everything was well. Some ministers who did not address their problems directly ended up with explosive issues that caused personal devastation.

One of my issues is depression. The illness of our son, David, exacerbated it. My belief that confessing my depression was tantamount to confessing that I was weak and incapable of solving my problems also made me feel worse. Of course, that is precisely the confession I needed to make. Walking toward my depression has allowed me to examine many other parts of my life and, hopefully, become more dependent on God in the process.

I recognize anxieties that stem from childhood. However, I also understand that "when I was a child, I thought as a child and acted like a child," but now I am an adult (1 Cor 13:11). When do I take responsibility for my behavior and my responses to life? Can I continue to say that because my father was an alcoholic, I am allowed to disrupt other people's lives with erratic and irrational behavior?

Obviously, these days we understand conditions like depression better than people did in the past. Depression has biological and neurological components. When we are truly depressed, it's not helpful for somebody to admonish us to get over it. Few people that I know choose to be depressed; it is a bleary existence.

The changing seasons of nature are sometimes used to describe personality types. For example, a "springtime" individual is by nature bright, optimistic and ebullient. A "wintry" personality, by contrast, is often melancholy, contemplative, and introspective. Wintry persons tend to be more sensitive to negative criticism, function with unrealistically high expectations of themselves and may feel anxious and depressed.

I have recognized in myself tendencies from various "seasons." Some serve me well, and some interfere with my connections with others and with my leadership. For example, I have the courage to speak out when I perceive something is unfair or needs changing. In some ways, this has served me well in my ministry.

I have tried to address changes that I consider necessary in a church or institution. For the most part, I have supported changes that have worked to the benefit of the group. The other side of this tendency is my difficulty accepting what people don't want to change or even acknowledging that my opinion is wrong and others are right. The fact is that some people either don't need to change or, if I think they do, they don't want to change.

A fundamental principle of leadership is the recognition that institutions and individuals are autonomous and don't need to be remade in my or your image. We offer our perspective on issues, but change is not forced.

Understanding both our strengths and weaknesses is essential to effective leadership. We become more coherent, integrated, and even healthier persons when we acknowledge that there are places where each of us is strong and where each of us needs to work to improve. We understand better our reactions to things that happen to us or to words that are spoken to us when we realize that we are mature in some ways but still growing in others.

My mother used to say to her two sons, "You're having growing pains." If we had a sore leg for no apparent reason, my mother explained, "It's a growing pain." I wanted to grow up, but as my mother reminded her sons, "Growing involves pain." Effective leaders recognize their growing pains and don't operate with unrealistic expectations about "pain-free" leadership.

As Henri Nouwen reminds us, being wounded is simply recognizing that we are human beings. Realizing that fact can allow us to connect with each other, to celebrate the gifts God gives to us, and then to accept the places where we are still being redeemed.

Few dangers are greater to the morale and the effective work of a community than someone who believes his opinions are always right. Recently, I heard about a church that was absolutely paralyzed by the contention between the pastor and one of the deacons. Both needed to be right on every issue, but as you can guess, they had diametrically different opinions on almost every matter. Because both of them needed to be right and to win, discussions degenerated into arguments, and the group process was co-opted by the egos of people who only wanted their agendas to prevail.

Being a coherent person is recognizing our strengths and weaknesses, staying open to those who remind us of our blind spots, and understanding that leadership is not always about winning. Dietrich Bonhoeffer, the German Lutheran pastor who opposed Hitler's pogroms and sought to have him removed, was killed by the Nazi regime before he witnessed the fall of that terrible time in the life of his country. Because of his opposition to Hitler, Bonhoeffer spent several years confined in a prison camp and unable to preach and teach freely as he felt called to do.

On the surface, it looked as if Dietrich Bonhoeffer had lost. Yet, he retained his integrity and the focus of his life. While Hitler deteriorated personally, Bonhoeffer maintained his coherence. At times, Bonhoeffer struggled with his circumstances, but he wrote poignantly,

> For the greater part of our lives pain was a stranger to us. To be as free as possible from pain was unconsciously one of our guiding principles. Niceties of feeling, sensitivity to our own and other people's pain are at once the strength and weakness of our way of life. From its early days your generation will be tougher and closer to real life, for you will have had to endure privation and pain, and

your patience will have been greatly tried. "It is good for a man that he bear the yoke in his youth" (Lam 3:27).[3]

Coherence means that the different parts of our lives come together so that what emerges is a quality marked by integrity and care for others. Coherence implies that we allow our sufferings and disappointments to tenderize us and to deepen us to our own dependence on God. Interestingly, the biblical word for "salvation" can be translated "wholeness."

Salvation is not simply life after death; it is also life after birth. Wholeness is the awareness that we are created and sustained by a loving God and that all of the events and occurrences in our lives can shape us to be kinder, sensitive, and more understanding of who God is and who we are.

Notes

1. Nancy Stanford-Blair and Michael H. Dickmann, *Leading Coherently: Reflections from Leaders around the World* (Thousand Oaks CA: Sage Publications, Inc., 2005).

2. Henri J. M. Nouwen, *The Wounded Healer: Ministry in a Contemporary Society* (Garden City NY: Doubleday and Company, Inc., 1972).

3. Dietrich Bonhoeffer, *Letters and Papers from Prison,* rev. ed., ed. Eberhard Bethge (New York: The MacMillan Co., 1967).

Chapter 3

Interpersonal Qualities of a Transformational Leader

The term "transformational leader" suggests that a leader not only *does* something but also *is* something. That's why it's important to begin with the character and values a leader possesses. Greek rhetoricians like Cicero and Aristotle talked about the centrality of "ethos" in communication, that is, the character of the person speaking. Was he ethical, authentic, caring, and trustworthy? Did the rhetorician embody the qualities that drew us to the person and made his comments credible?

What applies to rhetoric, or "preaching," as we call it in the church today, also applies to leadership. Effective leaders exhibit qualities like compassion, competence, and consistency, as discussed in chapter 2. These qualities help us hear what the leader is saying and feel that the leader has our best interests at heart.

While a leader is somebody we respect, she or he is also someone who relates to others. Relating effectively demands skill set that extends beyond the personal qualities of a leader and allows that leader to adapt to the needs and challenges of a particular situation. In his pacesetting work on "Emotional Intelligence" (E.Q.), Daniel

Goleman points out that an effective leader needs both "personal competence" and "social competence."[1] Personal competence involves "self-awareness" and "self-management." As Goleman states, "These capabilities determine how we manage ourselves."[2] Social competence includes the capabilities that determine how we manage relationships. Corresponding to personal competence, social competence includes "social awareness" and "relationship management," according to Goleman.

Goleman is aware that leadership is both who a person is and what a person does. For example, the first component Goleman includes under social awareness is "empathy." To Goleman, empathy is "The ability to sense how others feel and to understand their perspectives [and this] means that a leader can articulate a truly inspirational vision."[3] Without personal competence, however, empathy is difficult to achieve. A leader needs to possess emotional self-awareness and self-confidence, and out of those personal qualities flows the capacity to care for and be empathetic to others.

Thus, the whole concept of transformational leadership is built on the vital interplay of what we are becoming in Christ and how we seek to be transformative people in the places we are called to serve. Thus, an integral, inseparable connection exists between the personal and interpersonal components of a leader. With that assumption, I want to focus more specifically on what Goleman calls "social competence" and the *interpersonal* qualities of a leader: trust, communication, empathy, imagination, and transparency.

Trust

Trust in God

As a Christian minister, my fundamental focus is to call people into a relationship with the God most fully revealed in Jesus the Christ and to try to nurture that relationship in my preaching and teaching. But why is trust in God a necessary component in a leader?

The short answer is that a leader deals not only with ideas but also with people. If we take our best idea to a group of people, in most instances not everyone will see it as the "best" idea. Some may see it as a bad idea, an old idea, or an idea that should never be shared. In fact, some people may not discuss the idea at all. Some people may not hear the message, but they see the messenger. This is a hard reality, but some people may not like us and may resist our ideas for a host of reasons.

If you are like me, I see my ideas and opinions as an extension of myself. Having an idea is not unlike having a child. Being told that your child is ugly is not what you want to hear. Similarly, being told that the beautiful idea you conceived is unattractive has a way of making you defensive. Usually, this gives rise to conflict in the group, pushing the idea to the edges as individuals battle for power.

In the next chapter, I discuss how you and I can deal more effectively with the inevitable conflict a leader faces. Here, my focus is establishing a foundation from which to build our lives and with which we can better address our frustrations and even our failures.

Ronald A. Heifetz and Marty Linsky talk about the need for a leader to maintain a "sacred heart."[4] I first heard this term as I sat in Ron Heifetz's class at the Kennedy School at Harvard. Frankly, I was stunned that Heifetz began his discussion of leadership by stressing the importance of a "sacred heart."

I was surprised because I chose the Kennedy School in order to step away from the "Christian matrix" where I had lived most of my life and gain exposure to a more secular view of leadership. After all, among the approximate 100 students in the class, I was the only vocational minister. As I mentioned earlier, I thought I would need to "baptize" some of the ideas I heard in order to make them work in the church. However, when I heard Heifetz mention "sacred heart," I felt the waters lapping at the top of my baptismal waders.

I learned was that Heifetz was a devout Jew. While skilled in the techniques of effective leadership, Heifetz recognized the need for a leader to remain open and alive and not become jaded by the sometimes overwhelming demands that accompany courageous leadership. As Heifetz states, "The most difficult work of leadership involves learning to experience distress without numbing yourself."[5] When we lose our "sacred heart," enabling qualities such as innocence, curiosity, and compassion degenerate into cynicism, arrogance, and callousness.[6]

Marty Linsky, Heifetz's colleague in writing *Leadership on the Line*, relates a moving story about Heifetz and his wife Sousan. They attended a Jewish workshop on ecumenism. At the workshop, the speaker explained, "Sacred heart [is] . . . a reflection of God's promise, not to keep you out of the fire and water, but to be with you in the fire and water."[7]

When Ron Heifetz spoke to our class about the imperative of a "sacred heart," I was deeply moved. Even in the Christian circles in which my ideas about leadership were shaped, I never remember hearing about how a leader preserves his humanity and keeps alive a sense of wonder and even innocence. Leaders worked often with the thought of making life more humane and holy. However, with the pressures that come with bold leadership, the question is, "How does the leader maintain her sacred heart?"

As a minister, I talk often about trust in God. As my beloved faculty colleague Dan Goodman used to say, "How easy it is for us to use religious rhetoric but how difficult it is for us to practice what we preach." Little did those of us who taught with him at the Divinity School at Gardner-Webb University realize that this brilliant, caring New Testament scholar would have his life cut far too short. Yet Dan left us with the reminder that the important issue is to know the reality that our rhetoric tries to describe.

Where does the leader, or any of us for that matter, find something or someone whose love for us is certain and constant even when things around us are not what we may choose? Or, to put it another way, where does our confidence find a place that allows us to stand when our situation frightens us, discourages us, angers us, or makes us want to quit? We do have those moments. Others question and even reject our ideas. Because they are our ideas, we may take the negative criticism personally and feel attacked. The reasoning is that if you don't like my opinions, you must not like me.

Obviously, if we are to survive as leaders, we must avoid personalizing every negative word. Perhaps somebody in the group doesn't like us or doesn't like ministers or doesn't like people in positions of authority. We may remind someone of the cousin she never liked or, even more painful, our bright idea may not be as bright as we thought. It is humbling to watch our well-conceived plans disintegrate in the light of another's scrutiny. Some of us don't know when to compromise or to surrender because our sense of self is tied to what we want.

Leadership is becoming more democratized. As someone put it, the idea of the "alpha-male" who intimidates and dictates to others is being replaced by the will of the community. That doesn't mean a leader walks into a meeting with no aims or no agenda, but it does mean we need to welcome and honor the response of the community. Some of that response is well thought out and expressed in kind, considerate ways. Some reactions leave us wondering, "Where did that come from, and what did I ever do to offend that person?" This is called "human nature," and a leader needs to be comfortable in his own skin in order to respond and not react.

But where do we get that comfort and confidence? From ourselves? Left to myself, I can be as peevish, petulant, and defensive as anybody else I know. Does the confidence come from others? I am fortunate to have kind, caring people in my life who have supported and loved me even when I made mistakes. I have also worked with people, as you have, who make me feel less guilty when I draw my paycheck at the end of the month. If I look to find my confidence in the response of these people, I will wait for something that probably will never happen.

That brings us back to a sense of ourselves based in our trust in a loving God and our loving God's trust in us. As Parker Palmer writes,

> We must resist the popular tendency to think of transcendence as an upward and outward escape from the realities of self and world. Instead, transcendence is a breaking-in, a breathing of the Spirit of love into the heart of our existence, a literal in-spiration that allows us to regard ourselves and our world with more trust and hope than ever before. To experience transcendence means to be removed— not from self and world, but from the hall of mirrors in which the two endlessly reflect and determine one another.[8]

For much of my life as a follower of Jesus, I have seen my faith as a one-way street. Faith is how much I believe in Jesus; how closely I emulate his teachings; how faithfully I am the compassionate, caring person I envision Jesus was. However, I am constantly aware of the distance between what I want to be as Jesus' follower and what I actually am. That distance can become a constant source of frustration, sadness, and even despair. Simply put, I keep stumbling over myself as I try to follow the "via dolorosa."

I don't want to excuse my failings. Parts of me are still being redeemed, and I suspect that I will stumble over myself and into others as long as I live. While others may look to me as a minister and expect more of me than I can give, I try to see myself as a fellow pilgrim and a fellow struggler. As a preacher, I offer my words in the worship place. Hopefully, they are words that come from my encounter with the texts of Holy Scripture and from the Christ of God revealed in those sacred documents, but the words always come through me. I know what the Apostle Paul meant when he said God puts treasure into earthen vessels (2 Cor 4:7).

But to trust in God is not to trust in what I may believe about God; it's to reverse the equation and focus on what God believes about me. The incredible part of transcendence is that God pitches God's tent with me. Even more, this God mysteriously indwells and inspires our lives so that if it seems everything is taken from us, God never abandons us. As Parker Palmer says, ". . . transcendence is a breaking in, a breathing of the Spirit of Love into the heart of our existence . . . ."9

Leadership involves risk. The best leaders fail sometimes. Not everyone responds to a leader in a positive way. At times, even our best efforts, best thought, and best work are not sufficient to accomplish our goals. We are disappointed that we didn't achieve our purposes. That's the risk of bold leadership. We will succeed, and we will fail. Hopefully, our successes will outweigh our failures. Nevertheless, we need that sense of "transcendence." The great mystery of our faith is that an "Other" loves us not for what we do but for who we are.

Faith in Others

The "shema" of the Hebrew Bible that Jesus called the greatest commandment was to love God with all that we are and to love our neighbor as we love ourselves. Loving ourselves comes from the overwhelming realization that the caring Creator loves us unconditionally.

But the "shema" is not just about God and us; it calls us to include others in our care. How does that affect leadership?

First, a leader is called to help people be more of what God calls them to be and to try to make the world a more humane place. One day in class, Ron Heifetz was asked if Adolf Hitler was a good leader. Heifetz's response was an unequivocal "No."

On one level, we could make a case that Hitler was an effective leader. He galvanized a nation, rallied people with his powerful rhetoric, and certainly had a bold vision of conquest and making the "Third Reich" the center of the world. Hitler articulated his passion clearly and cogently. Unfortunately, his legacy still lives in the demented ideas of those who believe in "white supremacy" and who cherish the memory of their "Fuehrer." If leadership is simply the ability to rally people to a cause, then we have a long list of those who used their charisma and persuasive powers to leave us an unimaginably divided and twisted world.

Leadership is more than the capacity to create a following. What are we calling people to follow, and what are we asking them to be and to do with their lives? Is it to take the church, the institution, or the organization to the place where we see God at work in the world and join God in care for all of humankind? Too often, so-called leaders function by identifying the enemy and marshalling people against a perceived threat. For Hitler, the immediate enemy was the Jews, and now we live with the memories of families separated, gas chambers, and the horrific death of at least 6,000,000 people.

Some folks can energize people with their demagoguery and by identifying the enemy. All of us have convictions about issues, but to turn those convictions into hatred against a group of people is appealing to the worst instincts of tribalism, sexism, nationalism, or whatever "-ism" we identify as the enemy.

We now live in a global community filled with a variety of people, ideas, and religious persuasions. How do we negotiate this sea-change in our world's landscape? Differences are frightening. I turn on CNN and instantly see pictures of people who don't look like me, think like me, or necessarily have the same values as I do. Are these people "enemies," or are they God's creations? Will I make the world a better place through a crusade against those who are different or by calling myself and others to try to understand and to care for those who are different?

I'm not naïve. Our world is filled with people who define themselves by manipulation, intolerance, and hatred for people. Frankly, people whom I don't know despise me because I'm American or a Christian or whatever. I wished we lived in a world where we could sit down to talk and, if not love, then at least tolerate each other.

I'm not naïve about the church or a Christian institution. With few exceptions, most of us have some self-centeredness, and we are not always working for the good of God in our world. Some of us don't even recognize the ways that we jockey for position or power. I see in myself a need to control, and I don't like it when that need makes me fearful and anxious and causes me to try to outmaneuver those who have the same need to control.

Once in a while, however, I catch a glimpse of my better self. As a minister, I preach a sermon where I am less concerned about how I'm doing and more concerned about what God is doing in the lives of the listeners. I sit in a meeting and am less anxious about how I can interject my opinions and more open to hear what others say. I fly home from a meeting with a "little something" for each of my family, and it is a genuine expression of my deep love for them. I call a friend to check on how he's doing not because it's the "expected" thing to do, but because I genuinely care.

Examining my life helps me to relate to others because I understand that all of us are a mixture of mercy and meanness, selflessness and self-centeredness. Yet, God loves each of us. That love is a sheer gift. The challenge is to live with a gracious spirit toward others. Leaders are not called to put people down. We are called to lift people up to be whatever God gifted them to be.

Faith in others is inspiring others through our words and care so that together we can make at least our part of the world a better place. This assumes that a leader is secure enough with himself that he is able to share credit for a job well done and also assume blame in difficulty.

Frankly, this is tough for many who want to lead. Being negatively criticized is not enjoyable for any of us, but it's especially difficult when our sense of self is based on achievement and success. The counterpoint is a need to receive all the credit for success and none of the blame for what we perceive as failure. When the spotlight shines, we want it only to be on us.

The problem is that few of the things we accomplish are done in isolation. They are done in community. I look at my life, and maybe you look at yours. Whatever we are, it is not because we have made life's journey in isolation but because people have guided, nurtured, and invested themselves in us. For me, Bob Payne is one example. A young banker who was active in my home church, Bob poured his life into mine and helped me see my gifts. He took the time to affirm me. Parker Palmer captures the spirit of what I recall happening in my life: "A circle of trust holds us in a space where we can make our own discernments, in our way and time, in the encouraging and challenging presence of other people."[10] I needed to show up, and Bob Payne held me in the space of his affection. Then he blessed the person who showed up, and for that I will always be grateful.

A good leader trusts others, gathers around her those whose strengths supplement what she may lack, affirms these people as colleagues in the work, and knows how to share credit and bear blame. The intent of any organization is not to be a group of individuals bent on their own way and furthering their personal agendas. Rather, the purpose is to function as a team in which each person knows his job, supports others on the team, and is aware of the overall goals of the group.

This view of leadership finds strong support in the Bible. Moses gathered around him people like his brother, Aaron, who supplemented Moses' weaknesses and helped him lead the people out of bondage. Jesus had disciples, and while these men were seldom the paragons of virtue and commitment, they were an integral part of

Jesus' ministry. The Hebrew Bible centers on community, specifically the community of Israel. At the same time, the New Testament stresses the hallmark of community, namely the disciples and eventually the "ecclesia," the church. Narcissism or, on the other hand, self-doubt that can't include other people in the formation of community quickly chokes the morale of a group and keep people from ownership of the group's direction.

Communication

A second vital component in the interpersonal qualities of a leader is the ability to communicate with others. A leader must be able to fashion a clear vision for the organization. Before we can articulate an idea to others, we must articulate it to ourselves. What do we want the group to do, and how do we communicate this? Philosopher Franz Kafka once used the image of a man who jumped on a horse and rode off in all directions at the same time.

The danger of not being focused results in one of two equally disastrous results. The first is that we have no idea what to do in a particular situation. It's hard to give ourselves to nothing. The second is equally harmful. A person can have too many unformed thoughts and, like Kafka's character, he jumps on the horse and rides off in too many directions at the same time.

Listening

While communication is usually interpreted as what we say to others and how we say it, a vital step in effective communication is the ability to listen. Three factors are involved in listening. First, we need to listen to ourselves—our fears, biases, loves, and angles of vision. What somebody says to me is filtered through my experiences and values. That means I never listen in a pristine, pure way. I'm always interpreting what I see and hear. We need to pay close attention to what causes us to overreact, to stop listening, and to become closed-minded and defensive.

Second, we need to listen to the words somebody speaks. What is the person calling us to do? What is the person trying to do to us with his words? For example, some people are notorious for refusing to "own" their opinions and often say something like, "A number of us were talking, and we believe that you need. . . ." Sometimes it's helpful to ask a person who approaches us, "But tell me what you believe. I want to hear from you."

Third, as Ron Heifetz reminds us, we need to try to hear the music beneath the words. We need to listen to the "affect" or the "feeling" of the person who talks to us. When what we say is inconsistent with how we speak, confusion in communication results. If you ask me how I'm doing, I may say, "Fine." But how do I say it? What is my tone of voice? The music beneath the words can reinforce what I'm saying or, if the music doesn't fit the lyrics, the message may get confused.

Leaders need to remember this when they communicate to a small group as well as to a large group. Enthusiasm breeds enthusiasm. Competence creates confidence. Some people fine tune their messages but deliver them in a way that sounds like someone reading a laundry list. When Walter Cronkite, the famed newscaster, died in July 2009, United States President Barack Obama remarked, "He [Cronkite] invited us to believe in him, and he never let us down."[11]

Smiling at appropriate times is also vital to communication. A smile communicates warmth and intimacy. Along with eye contact, a genuine smile tells the audience that the speaker is not afraid of those to whom she speaks and is willing to engage the group with her ideas and with herself.

Speaking with Conviction

People who seek to lead need to believe that their ideas are important. Importance is not the same as perfection. We all need feedback of others, and in light of it we sometimes change our approaches.

However, if we are tentative in presenting our ideas, people will hear the uncertainty in our voices. Listen to some people speak and conclude whether they believe what they are sharing is important. Some people sabotage their ideas by constantly using phrases like, "Permit me to say this," "If you don't mind," or "I will try to get through this as quickly as possible." Other speakers lose conviction by constantly taking verbal excursions as if what needs to be said is not interesting enough in itself.

Near my wife's home in Kentucky is a road named "Zig-Zag." The road lives up to its name. Whenever I pass the road, I don't see many cars on it. I'm guessing that unless someone absolutely needs to take the road, nobody chooses to spend the gas to "zig-zag."

Speakers who constantly take "excursions" are the verbal equivalent of "Zig-Zag" roads. When people listen to a person in leadership, they expect precision of thought and clarity of expression. Occasional anecdotes or stories are good, but when these illustrations are not connected to the ideas, then people have a difficult time comprehending what someone is calling them to do.

If I believe that what I'm saying is important, I also want to get to it as quickly as possible. For those of us who preach, this has important implications for introductions to sermons. Many homileticians have taught that an introduction to a sermon should get people's attention. Often, this leads to a sensational story. While it gets attention, the problem is that when you tell a story that has listeners wide-eyed and sitting on the edges of their pews, how do you make the transition to the rest of the message? A good introduction is interesting, but it must lead naturally into what we want to say. Besides, if we are so concerned about a rousing introduction that causes people to listen, we say implicitly that our material won't keep people's attention.

Conviction is not a synonym for shouting or for imposing our views on others. A person who speaks with conviction doesn't have to be the most eloquent orator. However, the message finds its place within the deepest parts of ourselves, and we speak not just with our lips but with our lives.

Speaking with Courage

A leader calls people not only to maintain the status quo but also to make changes that make their part of the world a better place. While we like to believe we would change our views, opinions, and lifestyles in favor of a kinder, more compassionate world, we resist change.

Change is perceived as loss. We have to give up something. We have to give up the way we think, act, or process life. We get used to our ways, and when we are called to change, we may direct our grief and anger toward the person who asks us to change.

This is one of the heavy demands of leadership. We like people to respond to us positively. Unless someone enjoys "stirring things up," most of us like the water to be placid and people to feel comfortable. While this is an idyllic image, it is hardly a picture of what change entails. Change demands courage.

In calling ourselves and others to make changes, we need to remember certain things. First, we must call others to change in the context of respect and care for people. Most of us change when we are "loved" into change rather than being berated for our shortcomings. Anger is an appropriate emotion, but we must strive not to speak with an edge and sharpness that alienates people.

Second, we need to remember that, as mentioned earlier, many people often perceive change as loss. Therefore, a person may not resist the result of the change but the fact of changing. We become accustomed to thinking and doing *our* way. It is said that the seven last words of the church are "We have not done it that way!" Is this a result of obstinence? Perhaps. But it may also reflect that change causes disruption in our lives. We may actually grieve over what we "lose" in the process of changing.

Third, we may need to call for change incrementally. A sensitive leader recognizes when she calls a group to do too much at one time. A leader knows that if people are asked to make too many changes at once, he may create a situation in which people become immobilized and nothing ever changes.

Good leaders are *patient*, which is not an easy virtue. We sometimes want major change to occur by sundown tomorrow at the latest. However, that's not the way most of us make significant changes. Often the issue is whether we want to make a point or to effect real change. Real change requires patience with ourselves, with others, and with the processes through which ideas must travel in order to come to fruition.

With these caveats, leaders must be bold in their vision and courageous in calling people and institutions to change and to adapt. As Jim Collins reminds us, organizations need to move from good to great.[12] Some of us may need to move from living in mediocrity, doing business as usual, or being content with the status quo to making a difference in the world. Simply trying to keep the institutional boat afloat is far different from the kind of leadership that energizes people and seeks to make a positive difference in the world.

Ponder some of the problems our world faces: injustice, war, disease, poverty, a growing disparity between the haves and the have nots, climate change. We could go on and on! The point is that while we may not have the power to change everything, we do have the power to change some things. This is hardly the time for timidity. Leaders courageously give voice to their convictions and call others and themselves to the places where God wants to bring healing and restitution.

Empathy

The word "empathy" has a bad reputation. When the president of the United States nominated Judge Sonia Sotomayor to fill a vacancy on the Supreme Court, he said he looked for a person who was not merely an outstanding jurist but also empathetic. Almost immediately, opponents of the president's nomination seized on the notion of empathy. To some, empathy was antithetical to the idea of a judge who, in their opinions, needed to rule strictly on the law and not allow her "feelings" for any individual or group of people to influence her thinking.

The concept of empathy has been made to sound soft and subjective. Granted, there are standards by which to abide. For example, I don't expect to be excused from running a red light by telling the officer that I'm hungry and need to get home to supper. Rules and regulations are essential to the efficient operation of any group. Procedures and policies are important, and leaders must make them clear to those in the organization.

However, that doesn't eliminate the need for empathy, which is trying to understand another person, how that person thinks, and what influences the ways that person behaves. In fact, empathy, as

Daniel Goleman and others have reminded us, is absolutely essential to leadership.

Leadership involves working with people. Leaders may ensure that policies and procedures are followed, but they also recognize that people are different and that understanding those differences is vital to the morale and work of a group. Empathetic leaders know that each person is a unique creation of God; that we have both strengths and weaknesses; and that an organization functions much better when the members of that group interact with the leadership and receive respect as persons.

Imagination

Like "empathy," the word "imagination" probably sounds too indefinite to some people. This word is particularly troublesome to those who think concretely and tend to operate with a hierarchical view of leadership. A hierarchical perception is always conscious of who is in charge and believes ideas and information usually flow from the top down. Position in the organization equals authority, and people are reluctant to question those in the organization who possess the power. Frequently, a "go along to get along" attitude permeates groups like this.

Recently, I heard about a new pastor of a church who announced at his first staff meeting that he was the "chief." Apparently, this pastor was a fan of Western movies, so he chose the image of "chief." He might have chosen a different image, but his message would have been the same: "I'm in charge. Don't question my directives. I'll draw the map for the church, and everyone will go in my direction."

Criticizing this way of thinking does not imply that people in positions of leadership should avoid exercising appropriate authority. However, there is a difference between authority and authoritarianism. Authority connects with people and listens to their feedback. Authoritarianism isolates and insulates the leader and shuts down the feedback loop that is essential to the effective leadership of a church or any group.

How does this relate to imagination? Mature imagination operates in a communal setting. It trusts the dreams, desires, and insights that many people can bring to the shaping of an institution. Decisions are made in a corporate way and, therefore, are likely to be "owned" by those with an investment in the decision.

This doesn't mean a leader is devoid of ideas. No group wants the convener or leader to walk into the room and basically say, "Here's the challenge, but I have no idea where to begin." A leader brings her suggestions and ideas but refrains from imposing them on unwilling participants. Rather, a leader describes the challenge, offers possibilities for dealing with it, and then allows the group to respond and to react.

Imagination is not making something up or pretending that somewhere there is a wizard who can fix our problems. Rather, imagination is the ability to dream about and then visualize the possibilities of what we can do with God's help and our efforts.

Imagination can change a person or a group of persons, helping them re-envision their possibilities and stretch to achieve more than seems plausible. If reality is our only guide, we may never move beyond the routine. Most of us have attended meetings in which the voices of negativity took the wind out of everyone's sails. "We can't afford it; we don't need it; we have never done that before"—the litany goes on, and when these voices prevail, dreams die and the status quo lives.

This is not an appeal for reckless leadership that fails to ask hard, necessary questions before making a commitment. Instead, I think we need to let the imagination of the group loose so that we dream bold dreams.

We want to visualize how we can make a positive difference in the world before we decide in the first five minutes of the meeting that we don't have the resources to make any difference. Perhaps we will find that people commit to dreams that make a difference. The vision needs to be clear. Otherwise, people won't know what to follow.

Transparency

The final interpersonal component of leadership is transparency. In an excellent book, *Transparency: How Leaders Create a Culture of Candor*,

Warren Bennis, Daniel Goleman, James O'Toole, and Patricia Ward Biederman write about transparency in a system or organization:

> When we speak of transparency and creating a culture of candor, we are really talking about the free flow of information within an organization and its many stakeholders, including the public. For any institution, the flow of information is akin to a central nervous system: the organization's effectiveness depends on it. An organization's capacity to compete, solve problems, innovate, meet challenges, and achieve goals—its intelligence, if you will—varies to the degree that information flow remains healthy. . . . For information to flow freely within an institution, followers must feel free to speak openly, and leaders must welcome such openness.[13]

Unfortunately, some institutions develop a culture of secrecy. Sometimes this happens because the news isn't good, and the leaders believe certain information will damage the morale of the group. Obviously, not every piece of information is necessary to share in a public venue. The leaders may feel that particular points should be processed more or put in a larger context.

However, many of us who lead churches or organizations hide information because of our egos and the fear that it will reflect badly on us. If this type of secrecy becomes our "modus operandi," then people with a lack of information will imagine the worst. In the void of appropriate information, people wonder what's happening and usually conclude that the leaders are hiding something.

In this type of organization, two dominant responses from people usually surface. The first is anger. If an employee or volunteer fears that if he expresses himself, he will be terminated, his anger smolders as a burning kind of resentment. While not expressed to the people in leadership, his anger keeps him from feeling like part of the church or the institution. He may do his job, but there is no impetus for creativity, innovation, and doing any more than is basically required.

The second primary response is passivity. The desire to keep a job or stay in the good graces of the leader causes some people simply to accept mediocrity and live with it. The unstated rule of such organizations is that leadership is not receptive to different opinions or ideas, so the only response is "to go along to get along." This type of passivity is especially evident in the hierarchical style of leadership where knowledge and decision-making are concentrated in the hands of a few people.

This type of leadership not only discourages full investment of workers in the group, but it's also an implicit repudiation of the biblical notion that each of us is created and gifted by God. If a leader isolates herself because she is fearful that someone may challenge an idea or offer a different solution to a problem, that usually indicates that the leader is uncertain of herself and views other opinions as disloyalty rather than as a genuine attempt to help.

Theologically, it denies both the giftedness of the leader and the giftedness of all the people in the group. Transparency begins with the self-confidence that comes from knowing that we are never right about everything, but we are always right with the God who has created and sustains us.

Notes

1. Daniel Goleman, Richard Boyatkis, Annie McKee, *Primal Leadership: Learning to Lead with Emotional Intelligence* (Boston: Harvard Business School Press, 2004) 39.

2. Ibid., 59.

3. Ibid.

4. Ronald A. Heifetz and Marty Linsky, *Leadership on the Line: Staying Alive through the Dangers of Leadership* (Boston: Harvard Business School Press, 2002) 225–36.

5. Ibid., 227.

6. Ibid., 226.

7. Ibid., 228.

8. Parker J. Palmer, *A Hidden Wholeness: The Journey toward an Undivided Life* (San Francisco: Jossey Bass, 2004) 59.

9. Ibid., 53.

10. Ibid., 27.

11. Barack Obama, *Cincinnati Enquirer*, 18 July 2009, 1.

12. Goleman, Boytakis, McKee, *Primal Leadership* 34-69.

13. Warren Bennis, Daniel Goleman, James O'Toole, Patricia Ward Biederman, *Transparency: How Leaders Create a Culture of Candor* (San Francisco: Jossey-Bass, 2008) 3–4.

Chapter 4

Dealing with Conflict as a Transformational Leader

I can't speak for other ministers, but when I graduated from seminary, I had a grand illusion that everybody in the church would like me and like everything I did. Maybe some people outside the church wouldn't like me, but, after all, I could rationalize that. To the people outside the church, I saw myself as a prophet. I knew prophets in the Bible weren't always liked, but that's because they were so bold and courageous in addressing evil and injustice.

That was my illusion. The folks inside the church house would love me because we were a loving community of faith trying to change the world for Jesus' sake, and I was their pastor. Outside the church, some people might not appreciate me, but that was the price any prophet paid.

The thud you just heard was this "preacher-prophet" hitting the ground. You are not going to believe it, but not everyone on God's team appreciated the new quarterback. My illusion became disillusion. Why?

To begin with, I had misread the prophetic books of the Hebrew Bible. The prophets didn't have to go outside their houses of faith to find enemies. In their ways, the prophets criticized what they perceived as the spiritual failings of their own people. Few of us like to hear one of our own tell us we need to get right with God.

Not only did I not read the Bible right, but also I didn't read my experience with people in the church well. When my family joined a Baptist church, I recall a few church conferences in which the pastor heard from disgruntled members. Our deacons formed a welcoming committee at the front of the church each Sunday morning, and if you made it through the second-hand smoke and the snippets about the pastor and his boring sermons, you were ready for worship.

Also, when I was a seminary student, I served five years as the weekend pastor of Emmanuel Baptist Church, Rural Route 2, Lexington, Indiana. About seventy-five of the best people I've ever met made it to the church house each Sunday to listen to their young pastor and what passed for his preaching. The problem was that the folks at Emmanuel were too kind, and embedded in their psyches was the notion that if they criticized the pastor, God would visit all kinds of problems on them. I got away with "ministerial murder" because these folks were so nice or so frightened of God's wrath.

For example, one Sunday I preached a sermon on Jonah. I didn't prepare well, had no notes, and drew a mental blank as I preached. Throughout the sermon, I had Jonah wanting to go to Nineveh and avoiding Tarshish. I could see my wife, Diane, wince, but I couldn't figure out why this didn't sound right. If I had preached this at almost any other church, I would have had my bones picked clean at the back door. However, the kind folks at Emmanuel simply said, "That's all right, pastor! We changed the cities in our minds."

When I left seminary and encountered churches where people challenged me and criticized me, I thought for a while about a new, less public vocation. However, while the shape of my calling has changed from preaching to teaching and now to preaching again, I'm glad I stayed with it. I'm also glad I learned a few survival techniques along the way.

Get Over the Idea that You and I Don't Have Our Own Issues

Whenever something doesn't go well, I tend to blame others. It's called "scapegoating." Many of us look outside ourselves and fault others for what goes wrong. Of course, this is an easier route than taking responsibility. We've all seen it. Leaders blame people for not listening and following. People in the church, institution, or organization blame leaders for not being bold enough or giving the group a viable vision.

At times, all of this is true. Some leaders don't take risks or communicate effectively. Certain people in every group are difficult and always blame the pastor, president, or whoever is in charge. The problem is that this results in an institutional impasse. Nothing gets done except blaming each other for what has failed to happen.

In churches, this is a particularly troublesome issue. Unless we choose to be autocratic leaders, which I don't suggest, as ministers we want to provide leadership, and we want to listen to and respect the people in the church. This means collaboration, but the process of how to collaborate is not clear. Often, ministers get frustrated because they are asked to lead, but they feel checkmated by numerous committees, people who object to any new ideas, or a finance team that can kill any innovation by saying, "We don't have the money."

Healthy churches work hard to make this intrinsically difficult process work. However, too many churches settle for a stalemate where nobody is truly happy, and ministers either look for new churches or settle for trying to put the best face on a bad situation.

When I talk about transformational leaders coming to terms with their own issues, by no means am I suggesting that people who try to lead are to blame for everything that goes wrong. However, I'm not sure that anything will change until we make the journey inward and see the edges that sometimes sabotage our success.

For example, some of us expect too much of ourselves and others, and we constantly bump our heads on the high bar of frustration. Trying for excellence is admirable. Trying to call ourselves and other people to be and to do their best is commendable. But not learning to live without everything and everybody being precisely what we want can incapacitate us with anger or discouragement.

Obviously, wanting the best for an organization is good. Certainly, it beats the "head in the sand" attitude that some so-called leaders adopt because they don't want to deal with conflict or pay the price for making needed changes in an institution. However, being unable to settle for less than the best in every person or in ourselves is simply the recognition that none of us is perfect.

Those of us who identify ourselves as followers of Jesus the Christ often refer to our lives as a journey of discipleship. A disciple is a person who is taught, and in Jesus' day, that teaching occurred in a relationship with a teacher. Among other names given to Jesus was "Rabboni" or Rabbi. People related to Jesus as he traveled from place to place. Sometimes Jesus taught in formal ways, but often the teachings were related to events and experiences that the disciples and their leader encountered along the journey.

None of the disciples was perfect. In fact, at times Jesus must have wondered if anything he said was taking root. Yet, Jesus never excommunicated any of his followers for imperfection. The disciple who left, Judas Iscariot, went for reasons of his own.

However, when we envision the church or a Christian institution, we often view it through the prism of that brief moment of ecclesiastical camelot in Acts 2:42-47. Unfortunately, with this focus, students preparing for ministry are not equipped to deal with their own shortcomings and the church's failures. Sometimes the minister wants the church to be perfect or almost perfect to affirm for that minister that he has worth as a leader. The result is disillusionment, and many who drop out of ministry do so not because they don't have the gifts, but because they expect too much of themselves and others.

Perfectionism or expecting far too much of ourselves or others is one example of personal issues that inhibit our ability to lead effectively. Each of us carries personal idiosyncrasies that sometimes negatively affect our performances. In retrospect, I look at my life and ministry as a series of moves from one position to another. Why? I certainly can bless it by saying that God was leading me to another place each time.

While I believe that God leads, the fact is that, humanly speaking, I had a mixture of personal ambition and fear of failure. While I gave my best to one situation, frankly, I saw it as a stepping stone to the next level. Fortunately, I had some success as a pastor and preacher, and this seemed to open new doors. My longest tenure as a pastor was six years as senior minister at a church in Georgia.

When I left that church to make my first venture into teaching at a seminary, things were going well at the church. While I was tired from the emotional, spiritual, and physical toll of our son's illness as well as the demands of a large church, I probably could have taken some sabbatical time to try to regroup.

However, what also influenced my decision to leave the pastorate was a fear of failure. Did I see that clearly at the time? No. In retrospect, however, I understand that I feared success would turn to failure, that people would perceive that I was not nearly as confident as I appeared to be, and that it was better for me to "get out" rather than be "found out."

In my seminary church, one member didn't like sunny days because that meant it would probably rain the next day. "It's a beautiful day," I'd say. "Well, yes, but you know, pastor, that just means we'll have rain soon," she'd respond. I thought that was funny at the time. Here was a person who couldn't enjoy anything because she knew it wouldn't stay that way. I stopped laughing when I looked at my ministerial career and realized that I couldn't bide success because, in my mind, failure had to follow.

Of course, this prevented me from establishing the kinds of long-term relationships that were essential to transformational leadership. I functioned better when a church needed leadership in a crisis or when things had to be turned around, but I had difficulty with the "ordinary times." I equated those with failure because nothing exciting was happening and I couldn't see the "results" of my work.

These are some of the issues for me. As I've come to recognize these more clearly, I feel a mixture of regret and satisfaction. My regret is that my own fears kept me from living into some situations more fully and more deeply. I missed long-term friendships that come when you spend years with a group of people. At the same time, I believe I've been able to use some of my gifts for leadership in crisis management and in helping to turn some churches and institutions in a more hopeful direction.

The primary thing is for us to know ourselves and where we still need to be transformed. I am still bringing some of my fears to God to ask for the grace and courage to change. I'm trying to live more fully into the so-called "ordinary" times of life and understand that these may be the occasions when I see best my own longings and how God works.

Again, Parker Palmer, speaking of transcendence, talks powerfully about what a prayerful sense of God can do to transform our lives and see the "holy" in the ordinary. "To experience transcendence means to be removed—not from self and world, but from that hall of mirrors in which the two endlessly reflect and determine one another."[1]

Get Over the Idea That Other People Don't Have Issues

Conflict is difficult because people have different perceptions about the same subject. For example, a pastor friend of mine came to a new church. He didn't feel comfortable with the podium in the sanctuary, so without consulting any other church member, he changed the pulpit to one that was more congenial to his style. On the surface, this seems like a simple change. After all, the pastor is the one who preaches, and he needs a pulpit with which he feels comfortable.

What the new pastor didn't know was that the old podium was given as a memorial gift in recognition of a deceased member who was still well loved by the congregation. Additionally, the man's widow was a member of the church and felt hurt by the actions of a pastor she didn't yet know. You can guess what happened. What seemed to the new pastor to be a simple needed change became the occasion for acrimony.

Looking at the situation, we can make observations. The pastor should have consulted the leadership before he changed the furniture. Rather than simply replacing the center of the pulpit area, as he thought, he had replaced something to which a number of the folks had emotional attachments.

This is one example of how conflict develops. There is the "presenting issue." In the case of my friend, the only issue in his mind was changing pulpits. What he didn't know and needed to factor into his decision was the history that he disregarded, and the fact that what he did set in motion both the sadness and anger of those who felt that he was insensitive to the people with an emotional connection to the old podium.

Those of us who attempt to lead people step into a stream, and often we know little about the headwaters and the history of that stream's development before we moved into the flow. Few actions we take to try to change people, churches, or institutions are as simple as we perceive. We must consider history, emotional attachment, the loss some feel when something is altered, imbalance that occurs when the status quo is questioned, and so on with the components of change.

Consultants such as Peter Steinke often discuss our need for "homeostasis." Homeostasis is a sense of balance, of being comfortable with the way things are even if that's not the way things should be. Changes disrupt the homeostasis, and we feel "off-balanced." We will do almost anything to recover balance, even if it means getting rid of whoever calls us to change.

Steinke and others invite us to participate in "system thinking." As Steinke says, "System thinking considers the 'interrelatedness' of the parts. Instead of seeing isolated, unrelated parts, we look at the whole."[2] While systems theory is more intricate and involved with its own concepts and language, at a fundamental level it helps us see issues in terms of their connection with other issues and with the history of an institution.

It is usually not as simple as replacing one pulpit with another. When I walk into a situation to try to give leadership, I'm not walking into a group where the past is deleted and the issues resolved. Whether I realize it or not, I'm "typing over" things that are already written into the lives of the people, and, therefore, none of us speaks or listens without previous agendas affecting what we say and what we hear.

Leaders need to take time to listen both to the words and to the "affective" music that accompanies the language. We need to develop a group of trusted confidantes who can help us both to know and to interpret the issues of a church or organization. Before we race to make changes, we must consider how they will affect people's "homeostasis" and whether we are prepared to deal with the imbalance and loss that some folks may experience.

Recently, I became the intentional interim minister of a congregation in Charlotte, North Carolina. While small in number, the church possesses some of the kindest, most caring people that I have known. While I knew this church went through a difficult separation from its former pastor, I didn't anticipate the anxiety and distrust that this experience created for them. After about three months as their pastor, I preached the type of sermon that I have preached at almost every other church where I have served as pastor. I saw the sermon as a pointed, challenging message to the church. I called the church to reach out to the community and to begin to move away from the fear that seemed to have gripped them.

On Monday night following the sermon, I met with the church's transition team. After our prayer, a woman looked at me and asked, "Are you going to leave our church?" Several other members of the team said they interpreted the sermon as a threat, and it revived memories of their painful separation with the last pastor.

What was happening in that meeting? Probably a lot of things that I'm still trying to understand. However, I did realize that the congregation was not ready to hear what I said, especially not in the forceful way I said it. I had unknowingly displayed insensitivity, and some had heard my message as, "You shape up or I'm gone." I confess that for someone who has taught preaching to students, that was an uncomfortable, painful time for me. Some had heard what I didn't intend, and I apologized for the pain the message had caused them. At the same time, we had the chance to reflect on where they were, and as some of them said, on their "ultra-sensitivity." The bottom line is that the people heard my challenge sermon as a personal threat, and that they needed to face things that were making them overly anxious.

As our group talked, it became clear that the issue wasn't deciding the conflict in one party's favor. It wasn't about defending the sermon. Our conflict came because we were at two different places. Nobody was absolutely right or absolutely wrong. We both brought our own "stuff" to the sanctuary that Sunday, and now on Monday it was time to listen and to care for one another. When I left the meeting that night, I was emotionally and physically drained, but I felt that I had gained an understanding of this church that has informed my ministry and preaching.

Choose Your Battles

Most of us have only a certain amount of energy to deal with conflict. Unless a person is wired for battle, you and I can't live with the constant tension that comes from a life filled with successive conflicts. Somewhere we need breathing room, a time when we can back off to relax and renew ourselves.

Sometimes we don't have the choice of avoiding a conflicted situation. This may be why some of our best and brightest young ministers are avoiding investing themselves in the local church. They look at many churches and see far more conflict than they want to endure. Obviously, there are good examples of healthy and focused churches that strive to be the missional people of God. However, the stories are legion of congregations whose battle lines are drawn on issues such as worship style and doctrine, to name a few. Some ministers feel depleted because they move from one battle to the next with little time for personal renewal. On the other hand, people in the church complain because the performance of the minister is not up to their expectations.

My feeling is that before it is too late to redeem both church and minister, people need to engage in honest dialogue and even invite mediation from an outside party. Seminaries and divinity schools need to put more focus on programs and guidance for churches and ministers that are in the throes of conflict or see a potential problem developing. Most schools prepare a person for the initial season of her ministry. However, we must also strive to help ministers and congregations as they move through the other seasons of life. Most ministers and churches need guidance as they make adjustments to each other and as they do the difficult work of changing that is an inevitable part of life.

Despite any planning, even in the most sensitive and flexible churches ministers face conflict that is a part of a group's evolution. A wise leader deals with a problem before it becomes too large and cumbersome. Most of us in ministry are nice people. We want to treat others kindly, and, in turn, we want the favor of other folks. Unfortunately, this often creates avoidance of the tough issues. We pray about them, which is a great thing. We ask God to intervene, which is also wonderful. Even so, when these approaches keep us from carefully confronting situations and hoping that issues will resolve themselves, our "niceness" and "need to please" leads to more and bigger problems.

Sometimes, though, we can pace the number of conflicts that we face at one time. As ministers, for example, we are more than conflict managers. We preach; we counsel; we conduct weddings and funerals; and much of our ministry is spent in activities that extract energy from us. Few laypeople realize the toll that being a pastor takes physically, emotionally, and spiritually.

In ministry, there is nothing I would rather do than preach, but there is nothing I dread more than preaching. In his Lyman Beecher lectures on preaching, Gardner C. Taylor refers to Gene Bartlett's phrase, "the audacity of preaching." Then Taylor reminds us,

> The person who preaches is as guilty of the wrongs against God against which he inveighs as are those to whom he addresses his words. He cannot help feeling a deep embarrassment at the recognition that those who hear are likely to ask justifiably, "Who is he to talk? Listen to her! Can you imagine the nerve?"[3]

While I would still choose to minister and try to follow the call, I recognize at this point in my ministry just how demanding this call has been. I have tried to take it seriously, sometimes taking myself too seriously. I have worked hard, often at the expense of my family and my personal spiritual formation. I have fought good fights and not-so-good fights. In retrospect, though, if given a chance to do it over, I would pay more attention to what I never had the possibility to change. I would monitor myself better because at times I lost my spiritual compass. Nothing fatigues us more than running fast and not being sure where or even why we run.

View Conflict as a Part of God's Story

A vocational hazard of those of us who talk about God is that we don't listen well to God. Conflict diverts our attention even more from the source of life as we become preoccupied with personalities and problems. It creates an episodic view of life. I simply move from one thing to the next, and there is never a thread that connects each episode to another.

My father-in-law was one of the nicest, kindest people I've ever known. I only had one problem with him. During the time of the slide projector and slides, he would gather the family in the basement of his house to show his slides. I never enjoyed looking at slides, even when they were well presented, but he had a way of making it worse.

The slides weren't organized. There was a slide of my mother-in-law and father-in-law on vacation in Hawaii followed by a picture of cows in their pasture, then followed by a slide from the fund-raising supper at the volunteer fire department. Most of the family seemed content. They knew the pasture and firefighters. They could move among images of disparate places and experiences with ease. My father-in-law enjoyed the experience, even though I felt frustrated by the disconnection. When we went to bed that night, I asked my wife, "Why doesn't your dad put the slides in an orderly fashion?" I think Diane replied, "He likes it that way, and it's his slide show." She may have said something about my obsessive-compulsive behavior and that I needed a higher tolerance for chaos.

I do. I plead guilty to my need to have everything in its place and a place for everything. To me, a story has a beginning, a middle, and an end. Let's do Hawaii and then we'll look at the cows. After we've done those, we'll look at the volunteer fire department.

While the slide show in the basement was painful to watch, I made it through to the end and learned to endure other equally episodic slide shows. More importantly than a slide show is how we view the events of our lives, especially the ones that are difficult and may involve conflict. Is life simply one event after another, some we enjoy and others we endure, or is there some kind of plot through which Transcendence works? Is God able to take the most difficult, disappointing moments of my life and fold them into a narrative where I can believe that the Divine is at work? For many of us, Frederick Buechner offers perspective that allows us to "frame" the seemingly nonsensical parts of our lives and not succumb to the notion that life is episodic with no plot. In *The Magnificent Defeat*, Buechner writes about "The Annunciation to Mary":

> Every storyteller, whether he is Shakespeare telling about Hamlet or Luke telling about Mary, looks out at the world much as you and I look out at it and sees things happening—people being born, growing up, working, loving, getting old and finally dying—only then, by the very process of taking certain of these events and turning them into a story, giving them form and direction, does he make a sort of claim about events in general, about the nature of life itself. And the storyteller's claim, I believe, is that life has meaning—that the things that happen to people happen not just by accident like leaves being blown off a tree by the wind, but that there is order and purpose deep down behind them or inside them and that they are leading us not just anywhere but somewhere. The power of stories is that they are telling us that life adds up somehow, that life itself is like a story.[4]

Those of us who preach speak of the tragedies, the pain, and the conflict that the Bible clearly says is part of the human story. Yet that's not the whole story! The Bible also speaks of exodus and the resurrection. A transformational leader keeps the whole narrative in mind.

Understand the Way You Handle Conflict

In 1997, the Alban Institute published a booklet titled *Discover Your Conflict Management Style*.[5] Written by one of Alban's consultants, Speed B. Leas, this small document has become a seminal work in the area of conflict management. One of the most important parts of this document is an inventory we can take to determine our dominant way of handling conflict.

Leas briefly describes six different styles for managing differences: Persuading, Compelling, Avoiding/Accommodating, Collaborating, Negotiating, and Supporting.[6] While Leas makes the point that each of us has a dominant tendency, he's quick to say that in different situations, various strategies are required.

In a time of crisis when people are fearful, the leader may need to compel people to action. At other times when a group functions at a high level, the leader may choose to be supportive. The point is that no one style is right all the time. Yet, most of us have a style with which we are most comfortable. It's our "default setting," the one we go to because it seems to fit us. Of course, the problem with following our "default setting" is that it may not be effective for the situation or for the people with whom we work.

While some ministers handle confrontation well and can be persuasive and compelling, many ministers will do almost anything to accommodate or to avoid. One of the problems is that some people will take advantage and fill the void of leadership with their own exercise of power. That wouldn't be a problem if everybody in the church was emotionally healthy and concerned about what was best for the group. We are naïve to think that's the case. While all of us struggle with our own baggage, there are people in almost any institution who crave power and who will manipulate the process and other people for their own agendas.

Compounding the problem for churches is the issue of who has authority. In our best moments, we prefer not to think about issues of power and authority in the church of Jesus Christ. While we like to imagine a church where there is no intrigue, no manipulation, and no power plays, it doesn't exist. We can comfort ourselves by remembering that the history of our biblical faith is replete with examples of these qualities. Cain and Abel, Jacob and Esau, David and Bathsheba—shall we continue? The New Testament has James and John asking Jesus if they can sit at his right and left hands when he comes into glory. The ultimate insensitivity is that their request follows Jesus' words that he will soon die. Look at the churches in the New Testament. Would anyone want to be minister at Corinth? If you and I tried to help transform that congregation, we would hardly know where to begin.

Transformational leadership is not an easy process because most of us can justify our behaviors. After all, we say, "If I don't look out for myself, who will look out for me?" It would be nice if we did unto others as we want them to do unto us, but in our kind of world, that's an invitation for disaster.

Ministers are often caught between the pull of keeping a job and trying to address issues and people who create problems. Often, these folks wield inordinate influence in our churches. I sympathize with this dilemma. I was a pastor with a family that I loved and for whom I wanted to provide. I found it far easier to talk about courage than to exercise that courage.

However, the fact is that ministers or other leaders who always accommodate may keep a job but lose their souls in the process. Also, we abdicate our fundamental purpose as leaders. The church or group exists to make the world a better place. When the institution is conflicted and filled with seething resentment, it is impossible to move outside ourselves and make a difference in the world. All our energy is consumed with trying to maintain our equilibrium and to keep the church alive and afloat.

Probably, the way that many of us would like to deal with conflict is through collaboration. When people discuss and arrive at a decision together, they feel a sense of ownership in the decision and enjoy a greater "buy-in" to the process of actualizing it. Information is shared, and people feel that they know what is happening and that they have a part in both formulating the dream and fulfilling it.

In most organizations, there is a "chain of command" or at least an organizational structure that details who is responsible to whom. This type of structure is helpful or hurtful depending on how it's used. If the leader sees it as a way to isolate and insulate herself from everybody but a handful of people, many creative ideas will be lost. Also, if the leader sees the structure as a way to impose his will on everyone else, that leader runs the great risk of sapping the morale of the group. Some people are content to be passive spectators of others' actions, but people with ideas and a desire to help the group will become quickly frustrated in such an environment.

As a minister, particularly in my Baptist tradition, I am concerned about the style of leaders that we are producing for our churches. Some are autocratic. Some have the charisma and personal appeal to make things happen the way they want. These churches seem on the surface to be free of conflict because the pastor is perceived as the winsome voice of God. However, some of them have great difficulty when that pastor leaves or retires and is followed by an equally autocratic pastor who lacks the personal qualities and the trust of his predecessor.

At the opposite end are ministers who fail to exert meaningful leadership. These ministers refuse to address issues because they have been taught that the church is responsible for finding its own direction. We must move toward a vision of leadership that empowers people to work together and also empowers ministers to have the courage to call the church to bold and meaningful ministry, even in the midst of conflict.

Notes

1. Parker J. Palmer, *To Know as We Are Known: Education as a Spiritual Journey* (San Francisco: Harper, 1993) 13.

2. Peter L. Steinke, *How Your Church Family Works: Understanding Congregations as Emotional Systems* (New York: Alban Institute Publication, 1993) 3.

3. Gardner C. Taylor, *How Shall They Preach: The Lyman Beecher Lectures and Five Lenten Sermons* (Elgin IL: Progressive Baptist Publishing House, 1977) 29.

4. Frederick Buechner, *The Magnificent Defeat* (New York: Seabury Press, 1979) 59–60.

5. Speed B. Leas, *Discover Your Conflict Management Style*, rev. (New York: Alban Institute Publication, 1997).

6. Ibid., 4.

Chapter 5

Preaching and Transformational Leadership

For much of my ministerial life, I have been either a pastor/preacher or a teacher of preaching. Preaching and leadership share one important thing in common. Both are arts rather than sciences. In both preaching and leadership, common denominators seem to move us more toward excellence, but there is not a common mold into which we can pour everyone and make us all excel.

Much of the excellence of preaching and leadership is in the eye of the beholder (or the ear of the listener). Like walking into an art gallery, our eye falls on a picture we like. It reminds us of a warm memory or a time when life seemed good, when people sat around the table eating and enjoying each other's presence. As we savor the picture, a stranger walks up beside us, looks at the same picture, and caustically observes, "That's maudlin!"

When Ronald Heifetz writes about leadership, he uses the term "adaptive." Heifetz distinguishes between "technical" problems and "adaptive" challenges. Technical problems are much easier to handle. If my computer isn't working, I call someone who knows something about computers, and that person fixes it. Adaptive challenges are murkier. They don't have a "quick fix," and therefore the leader has to decide among options. Heifetz rightly observes, "Leadership is an improvisational art."[1]

Preaching falls into the same category. The teacher of homiletics faces the challenge of a variety of students, different backgrounds, genders, races, and personalities. While stressing that some things are important, the wise teacher realizes that proclamation is not one size fits all.

When I was fifteen, I preached my first sermon at the Rescue Mission in downtown Miami, Florida. Men came into the shelter from the streets looking for a meal and a cot on which to sleep. Before they could get to the meal and the bed, these men had to listen to me. I'm sure some of them wished they had stayed on the streets.

In one of my first sermons, a man raised his hand to ask me a question. I was simply trying to make it to the end of the sermon without collapsing. I had never seen anybody raise his hand during a message to ask a question. Preaching is monologue. If you don't understand, don't ask me to explain! I spoke louder, but his hand stayed up. Finally, I stopped and asked him what he wanted. He asked, "How can you come here and tell us what to do?" He had every reason to wonder how I could come to a rescue mission and speak with any relevance to people whose lives were so different from mine. I was young, inexperienced, and naïve.

It's been a long time since that night at the Miami Rescue Mission, but the man's question has haunted me throughout my ministry. Who am I to preach to anyone about anything? What do I know about some people's lives? How can I preach to others when I know that often I don't hear my own messages and struggle with issues that I seem so sure about in the pulpit?

In many ways, the question of that man at the beginning of my preaching life has stayed with me and kept me humble. Yet, preaching is important to me, as imperfectly as I do it. With all my heart, I believe in the power of God to use words to help to transform our lives.

The Theology of Preaching

Probably no single person has had more influence on the shape of proclamation in our generation than Fred Craddock. One of his books, simply titled *Preaching*, speaks about a minister's need to have a theology of preaching. Craddock distinguishes between a "theology for preaching" and a "theology of preaching." A theology *for* preaching includes the theological beliefs that guide a preacher as he moves into a biblical text and seeks to bear its message to the listeners. For example, a certain text may lead us to speak about God and what we believe God can do in the lives of people.

A theology *of* preaching is what we believe happens in the preaching event itself. Do we believe the Spirit of God can take the gift of the words we offer and use it to transform lives? Or do we believe that preaching is basically a waste of time and that the last thing people want or need is more words?

Craddock believes deeply in the ability of speech to transform the lives of listeners. As Craddock states, "preaching is understood as making present and appropriate to the hearers the revelation of God. Here revelation is used not in the sense of content, although content is certainly there, but in the sense of mode."[2]

What does Craddock mean by the revelation of God both in "substance" as well as "mode"? To Craddock, the revelatory nature of sharing a biblical claim involves not only stating the claim of the text but also taking seriously the mode or literary form in which the text is couched. Rather than seeing the Bible as a "flat" document with sixty-six books, Craddock prods us to understand the way in which the revelation is stated and how that affects the substance of a biblical passage and how we hear that text.

Craddock especially encourages those of us who preach to think in terms of how much of the Bible is presented in stories and how we need to preserve that story quality in our preaching. Not long ago, Don Hewett, longtime and successful producer of *60 Minutes*, was asked why this show had been so successful for more than forty years. Hewett responded that he could summarize the reason in four words: "Tell me a story."[3] According to Hewett and Craddock, people don't want to hear just the facts or the conclusions; rather, hearers want a person, a face, someone who is involved in the situation, to help them fashion the story for themselves.

For Craddock, it is important that a preacher see the "present" of the Bible. If all the preacher does is "homiletical excavation," the impression is that the Bible was once in time a potent document, but is largely irrelevant for us today.

When I was about ten years old, and my parents had yet to make a commitment to the church, I recall one Saturday afternoon when a local Baptist pastor made a surprise visit to our house. We knew who he was because we had attended his church. On the coffee table sat a large family Bible that our family had purchased from a traveling salesperson.

The cover of the Bible was dusty because we seldom opened it. In the time it took for that minister to walk from his car to our front door, my mother had cleaned the Bible. When the minister came in, my mother proudly showed him our "dust-free Bible." Of course, he probably wasn't fooled because it looked too clean to have been touched.

Many Bibles are venerated but untouched. As a preacher, it is imperative to open a biblical text and, through her encounter with that word, to allow it to live both in her and in the hearers. For me, the preaching moment is full of possibilities. I deeply believe that, through the power of the Spirit of God, what seems old and dusty on the surface can become the present, transforming word of God.

The Transformed Preacher: Listening to What We Speak

One of the terms frequently used to describe a type of leadership is "servant." James Autry, in his book *The Servant Leader*, delineates six characteristics of this type of leadership:

1. Leadership is not about controlling people; it's about caring for people and being a useful resource for people.
2. Leadership is not about being boss; it's about being present for people and building a community at work.
3. Leadership is not about holding on to territory; it's about letting go of ego, bringing your spirit to work, being your best and most authentic self.

4. Leadership is less concerned with pep talks and more concerned with creating a place in which people can do good work, can find meaning in their work, and can bring their spirits to work.

5. Leadership, like life, is largely a matter of paying attention.

6. Leadership requires love.[4]

All of these qualities are vitally important to transformational leadership, but I am fascinated by Autry's observation that leadership is "a matter of paying attention." Being still, listening, or paying close attention have never been easy qualities for me to actualize. Being a verbal person, I'm more at ease when I talk instead of listen. When I'm in a conversation, I have to restrain myself from interrupting the other person. I can sense my anxiety as I begin to think, "You've said enough. Time is precious. Even though you haven't finished talking, I understand the issue. Furthermore, I can't wait to tell you the answer."

I know envy is not a good quality, but I envy contemplative types who know how to be still, listen, and observe. I have a friend whose hobby is ornithology or bird watching. He says his wife and he can spend hours quietly in the woods looking for different types of birds. As I listen to him talk about bird watching, I feel physical pain! On one level, I need to go to the woods and be quiet, but on the other hand, I would go crazy if that were my only option for a hobby.

Thus, listening carefully is not among the good qualities that come naturally to me. I suspect many of us in ministry are like that. Despite our training in pastoral care classes that taught us how to listen, and in spite of our wonderful models in spiritual formation groups, listening is still an art to cultivate.

The simple fact is that no one who preaches worthwhile sermons over any length of time does so without paying attention to events, people, and most of all to the biblical texts. Creating sermons is not the purpose of preparation. We listen carefully and lovingly to the voices around us, to the voices within us, and we speak authentically about the rhythms of life where God speaks. We either hear or we don't hear because we've stopped listening or maybe God has become silent.

In 1991, I spent a fall sabbatical with Fred Craddock at the Candler School of Theology at Emory University in Atlanta, Georgia. What I saw in Craddock and tried to learn for myself was more than I could possibly name. But the one thing that stands out was the way he listened to both the substance and the style of the Bible. Craddock, from his days as a college student at Johnson Bible College in east Tennessee, had an intimate knowledge of the Bible itself. He combined this with a strong understanding of critical methodologies that increased his appreciation for the Bible, expanding it with more depth and breadth.

A preacher tries to meet a biblical text again for the first time. Instead of encountering a familiar text and nodding our heads as if it's an old friend about whom we know everything, the proclaimer meets it again for the first time. For example, if I wish to preach from Psalm 137, I need to listen to it and let the words of the psalm begin to transform me. The first four verses of this psalm set the tone: "By the rivers of Babylon there we sat down and there we wept when we remembered Zion. On the willows there we hung our harps. For there our captors asked us for songs, and our tormentors asked us for mirth, saying, 'Sing us one of the songs of Zion!' How could we sing the LORD's song in a foreign land?" (NRSV)

Even if I know nothing about the historical setting of Psalm 137, I know a lot simply by reading and trying to experience these words. People are dislocated. They weep because they have lost something important. Instead of sympathy, they are tormented by their captors to sing through their tears. Then the question that summarizes the "feel" of this psalm rises from the troubled community: "How could we sing the LORD's song in a foreign land?"

Without turning to any commentaries, I begin to let these words wash over my life. I am a pastor, and the people look to me for a transforming word. I look for something that can transform me. Perhaps I begin by saying that even though I've never sat by the rivers of Babylon and certainly have never hung a harp on a willow, I know the feelings of loneliness, desperation, and even the sense that I can no longer sing the song of God.

I have been there, and so have some of my listeners. Consider the church where I am the intentional interim pastor. Many of the older people remember the warmth of a sanctuary and days when the church seemed so vibrant. Now we meet on Sunday mornings in a rented high school auditorium, and some wonder if the church will survive.

As their pastor, I want to give them a sense of hope. I want to say that God can change all of us, and I do say that because I believe it. But saying something like, "Don't worry; be happy," is foolish. The congregation is wounded; some are disheartened; many are tired from too much conflict. Transformation for our church will be incremental. It will require all the patience we can muster. We can recall other moments in our lives when we put the harps in the willows. We didn't want to sing, but God gave us a new song in the foreign land. Being a transformational leader does not mean we live somewhere other than the rest of humankind. It means that, even in our woundedness, we try to give ourselves and others a frame to put around what they experience.

Once we encounter the biblical text itself, we turn to the commentaries and other helps to enlarge and enrich our encounter or to correct misimpressions. We quickly discover this is a psalm sung as a lament. The people of Judah were taken into Babylonia. They were in exile. The temple was destroyed. Jerusalem was in ruins. Why would God allow such a thing? Or maybe floating through their minds was the notion that if a nation was defeated, it meant that its God was too small or even nonexistent. To what, if anything, do they now turn for strength?

A psalm is a song, but these people don't feel like singing. Or if they do, it's not going to be a song like "Blessed Assurance." It will be in a minor key, filled with questions and grief. While all of us treasure moments when the presence of God swells up like a giant wave and we sing with assurance and faith, God seems to accept our songs regardless of the music and the lyrics. In fact, if we read the final verse of Psalm 137, the exiled community sings about their despised captors of Babylon, "Happy shall they be who take your little ones and dash them against the rock!" (v. 9). How many sermons have we heard about these intensely vindictive words? The psalms seem to portray a God who cares for us when even in our hurt and rage we imagine things that in our best moments we would never consider.

While the psalms are lyrical, they are also part of the community's liturgical prayers. We bow our heads as we listen and are impacted in our lives by what others have said to God. As Tom Long reminds us in his comments about Psalm 1,

> The rhetorical effect of the poetry of the psalm, then, is to create two contrasting spheres of activity in the awareness of the reader or hearer. One sphere is filled with frenetic, desperate, directionless motion which quickly fizzles out. The other is still, steady, rich with the quiet and strong action of the wise person reflecting upon the Torah. An effective sermon on this psalm may well be one which not only *describes* this contrast but also *recreates* its visual and emotional impact in the hearers.[5]

As preachers trying to lead people, we experience the rhetorical impact of the text. We realize that we live in a world with two spheres. There is the "seen" world often filled with frenetic activity and countless meetings. We feel the drain on our energy and wonder if life is simply enduring one thing after another. Then we draw back to look at how we live. As Ron Heifetz observes, we move to the balcony to see if the dance of our days and nights has any real joy and purpose.[6]

Leadership is bringing ourselves and our hearers to what Heifetz calls the "balcony" and to what Long refers to as the other "sphere." In those moments when we get perspective and as preachers are able to offer perspective and purpose, then we know the real meaning of leadership.

The Transformed Hearer: Listening for the Voice of God

I find it difficult to write about listening to God's voice. A certain level of piety seems too sure of itself for my liking. People say, "God told me to do this." Suddenly, the distance between the Holy One and humanity collapses. When I was younger, I remember a popular bumper sticker that read, "God said it. I believe it. That settles it." These words were about the Bible, and I wished they were indeed the last word about the sacred book. However, we must remember Paul's words in 1 Corinthians 13:12: "Now we see through a glass darkly." We can't possibly know all there is to know about God and the Bible.

So I use the phrase "the voice of God" carefully. Perhaps God gives some folks the gift of keen hearing. Nothing is muffled. No interpretation is needed. Does God speak so cleanly and clearly to certain people that they know that everything they do and say is God's will? Unfortunately, I have not experienced that level of communicative clarity. I try to listen in the busyness and chatter of life to whispers, impressions, stillness, and even the chatter itself and pray that it is the voice of God and not an echo of my desires and needs.

While I don't hear God audibly and while there is always a degree of uncertainty in trying to interpret God's purpose, I still believe in the power of God to change and direct our lives. Preaching is one of the ways in which God can speak. I would have forsaken proclamation long ago if I didn't believe that the Holy Spirit often shapes us through the vessels of our lives and words.

For me, this change happens in two fundamental ways. First, God calls us to change from the inside out, and then God calls us to make a difference in the world. In essence, God calls us to change life from the outside in.

Hearing God: Changing from the Inside Out

I grew up in a faith tradition that put a premium on a person's change as an individual. This came as a call to salvation. The assumption was that each of us is alienated from God, but this God as revealed in Jesus' life, ministry, and especially death and resurrection desperately wants us to come back and be reconciled to the Divine. Preachers called us to confess our sins, repent or turn away from the way we lived, and believe in Jesus the Christ.

We were called to follow Jesus, although I recollect that discipleship or following was not stressed nearly as much as the experience of faith in Christ. Dramatic stories were told of people who died not believing in Jesus and thus spent eternity in hell. Obviously, we wanted to go to heaven, and we learned that where we spent eternity depended on whether we believed or didn't believe Jesus was the Son of God.

While I now view that kind of preaching as overly simplistic and ignoring the biblical call to justice, I am grateful for the foundations of my faith. While some of my ideas and much of my language have changed, I still deeply believe that Jesus calls people. While the group of Jesus' first disciples are known as the Twelve, these disciples are all named. Three of them, Simon, James, and John, occupy a prominent place in the four Gospels. Their struggles to appropriate what Jesus can do to change their lives are some of the most graphic episodes in the Bible.

In retrospect, I am grateful for those ministers who called me to the transformed life. While my pastors and visiting evangelists never talked about transformation, they couched their invitation in words and phrases like "saved" or "coming to know Jesus as your personal Savior and Lord." This was called evangelism, and the idea of "reaching people for Jesus" was the overwhelming priority of my church.

Recently, I met with a group of moderate Baptist ministers who wanted to talk about how their churches could reach more people. Some of their churches had plateaued in membership growth, and others were in slow decline. "How do we do evangelism when that word has been so distorted by misuse and abuse?" they wondered. "We want to reach people, but our theology won't allow us simply to come to Jesus without any deeper understanding of what that means."

Many of today's ministers face this conundrum. They know what they don't like. They don't like what Dietrich Bonhoeffer once termed "cheap grace." These ministers want to bring people to faith in Jesus as the fullest revelation of God, but their integrity and sense of the depth of God's call prevent them from inviting people to "be saved," since it often becomes the extent of the invitation. As Ron Heifetz probably would say, "We face an adaptive leadership challenge." This has no technical answer, and it poses a creative challenge for those who want to keep evangelism but deepen the notion of what it means to follow Jesus.

In my opinion, discipleship has to accompany evangelism. In the New Testament, there is an initial moment when a person's eyes are opened to something of who Jesus is (for example, Simon Peter or Paul). We may call that the first step, but it is only the first step. The call to follow involves an initial "yes" along with a series of other "yeses," as we get to know more of who Jesus is.

Bill Hull, a former New Testament professor of mine, writes about what he sees as a significant gap in the available homiletical material.[7] Hull observes that virtually none of the numerous books and articles written in the area of preaching deal with the marriage of leadership and proclamation. Hull, who has experience as both an academician and a ministry practitioner, offers helpful advice about how to redress this deficiency.

In one section of his book, Hull speaks about "The Church as a Pilgrim People." About discipleship, Hull writes,

> What does it mean for the New Testament to define the Christian life as "follow[ing] in his steps"? It means that discipleship is viewed not as a noun, but as a verb. We are not called to *be* followers but to *do* following. Again, for the one so summoned, the offer is empty of human content. The command to follow conveys no ideas, arouses no feelings, describes no activities. Rather, everything depends on what the leader will do next, which makes the imperative "follow me" entirely future facing. It sets the respondents in motion, turns their lives in a new direction, and invites them to a succession of surprises. Further, it is only in such a venture that the follower discovers who the leader really is.[8]

Under the rubric of "pilgrim people," Hull offers ministers the opportunity to redeem the word "evangelism" and to feel good about its use. Rather than surrendering a strong biblical word to those who, in our opinions, cheapen it, let's take some hints from Bill Hull and use the word in a way that emphasizes the good news:

1. We are called to be followers, not to make a decision that doesn't take root in our lives. As Hull stresses, we are not followers in name only; we are committed to follow with our lives.

2. We are called to follow the leader. This involves trusting ourselves to the Christ we follow. We move into the future, but we don't know the future.

3. We are called to know this leader more by following him. Discipleship is a "venture" of trust, and through that trust and obedience to follow, we know Christ better.

Hull calls us to see that our "venture" in faith begins with a moment in time when we say "yes" to following Jesus. It's more, however, than merely acknowledging in our minds that Jesus is central. Rather, it's the commitment of all that we are to a relationship in which we seek to follow him and in the process come to know him more intimately. We follow him with the community of faith and, thus, we are the "pilgrim people of God."

This is both a call to *metanoia* and to *ecclesia*, to repentance and change and to community and church. As the pilgrim people of God, we continue to be changed from the inside out. When Paul wrote to the churches in Galatia, he named what he called the "fruit of the Spirit." Paul said, "the fruit of the Spirit is love, joy, peace, patience, kindness, generosity, faithfulness, gentleness, and self-control" (Gal 5:22, NRSV).

Part of the task of preaching is to call all of us to realize the possibilities of our faith. Ministers come with their own anxieties and anguish, and they preach and listen to their message on the peace that the Spirit of God can give. Hopefully, our eyes and ears are opened to realize and receive the gift of God's peace. We come with the fretfulness that everyone does not respond to our ideas the way we want, and we preach and listen ourselves as we pray for more patience.

Granted, this type of preaching can become tragically self-centered. We can distort it into a "what's in it for me" kind of gospel, which is no gospel at all. We are not talking about bigger houses and better cars. We are talking about becoming more of what God calls us to be so that we can be more of God to others. To use the terminology of the Hebrew Bible, we are blessed by God so that we can bless others.

Hearing God: Changing from the Outside In

The preacher is called not only to proclaim a gospel of transformation to individuals but also to preach the good news to her community and to the world. In the ministry of Jesus, we see the strong emphasis on care for the outcast and the oppressed. While Jesus never became the militantly messianic figure calling Israel to triumph over the power of its Roman occupiers, he expressed deep concern for those who were marginalized in his day.

Perhaps that's the reason why some who have written and spoken most cogently about systemic issues in our day are those who would have been considered marginalized not long ago. Lyrically gifted and strongly articulate African-American ministers like Martin Luther King Jr. championed the rights of people of color and drew attention to all who were economically disadvantaged. In fact, King was assassinated in Memphis, Tennessee, in April 1968, where he had gone to lead marches and speak against the economic deprivation of the sanitation workers in that city.[9]

Feminist theologians such as Rebecca Chopp have also called the church to see itself not as a collection of individuals with needs but as a community of faith called to address the injustices of society. In her book, *The Power to Speak*, Chopp offers a needed perspective on proclamation:

> Such a task, the task of resisting and transforming modernity through discourses of emancipatory transformation, leads back to a reconsideration of the first focus, proclamation as constitutive of community. To form Christianity as a proclamation of this Word and words of resistance and transformation, as discourses that suggest new ways to speak of freedom and new attitudes and practices of being human, requires an emancipator transformation of Christianity.[10]

There was a time when voices like those of King, Chopp, and many others would not have been invited to the table where white male homileticians and theologians controlled the conversation. Now they remind us that the thrust of preaching is about both transforming people as persons and transforming the world for which God cares so deeply.

In our day, we face a serious challenge to the prophetic thrust of proclamation. Articulate, charismatic preachers dominate the media, espousing a message that God wants the best for everybody. It's appealing. In a time when people's minds are dominated by economic concerns and the challenges facing them and their families, we hear the voice of an attractive pastor telling us to be upbeat and that God will bring us through the storms.

In one sense, those who may view the preaching of people like this as thin gruel substituted for the gospel of self-sacrifice must at least acknowledge its appeal. At the same time, we have to ask ourselves, "What is the good news that we preach?" If the church is indeed the "pilgrim people of God," then what gives the pilgrims the purpose and passion to make the journey?

While it's easy to criticize those who preach a message designed to make people feel empowered, the real question is, "What am I offering in my proclamation that offers power (*dunamis*) to people?" Annie Dillard observes, "The secret of seeing is, then, the pearl of great price. . . . I return from the same walk a day later scarcely knowing my name. Litanies burn in my ears; my tongue flaps in my mouth, 'Ailinon, alleluia!' I cannot cause light; the most I can do is to try to put myself in the path of its beam."[11]

This is the Annie Dillard who told us that if we truly understood the explosive nature of worship, we would fasten ourselves into the pews with seatbelts. The order of worship where I preach offers no words on how to fasten seatbelts, much less on "litanies burning in our ears" and our tongues "flapping an alleluia." Most of my instructions about worship are much more prosaic: things like "Turn off your cell phones" and "Please take your children to the bathroom before the service begins."

I don't like proclamation that is intended to make me feel better or make me more optimistic in a world full of pessimism. Yet, I find myself too often approaching the pulpit with little sense of anticipation and alleluia. Can I blame people who are eating the wrong spiritual food if my own food has little taste in my mouth?

Perhaps, a response is found in the poetic, imaginative way that people like Annie Dillard offer us. After all, it's the way much of the Bible comes to us. Imagine ourselves as the pilgrim people of God. Alleluia! Imagine ourselves being transformed into more loving, caring people. Alleluia! Imagine ourselves living, preaching, and doing whatever we do not to make God love us but because we know God made us in love. Alleluia! Imagine looking at the world the way the Holy One looks at it. We love the world because God loves it, and we love people because God loves them. Alleluia!

Suddenly, we see the greed, the abuse, the injustices, the misuse of creation of which God has made us stewards. We are propelled to speak and to act because love demands it. The purpose of our proclamation is not to berate people, but to call us to imagine the world that God has always imagined. Alleluia!

Several years ago, I made my first trip to the Holy Land. I refrained from buying many souvenirs because for me that seemed to cheapen something profound. However, I did buy a banner with a picture of a lion and a lamb lying peacefully next to each other. Underneath are the words of the Psalter that calls us to imagine a new world: "I will lie down and sleep in peace; for you alone, O LORD, make me to lie down in safety" (Ps 4:8, NRSV).

Some see words like this as a promise for the future when God reigns and violence is no more. I suppose none of us will see the final end to war, homelessness, poverty, ecological destruction, and a host of other problems we face. Those of us who preach, however, are never promised success. Our call is to care and to be faithful. We are poets with imagination, and for that we may pay a heavy price. But if litanies burn in our ears and our tongues flap faithfully in our mouths, then Alleluia!

Notes

1. Ronald A. Heifetz and Marty Linsky, *Leadership on the Line: Staying Alive through the Dangers of Leadership* (Boston: Harvard Business School Press, 2002) 73.

2. Fred B. Craddock, *Preaching* (Nashville: Abingdon Press, 1985) 51.

3. "A Tribute to Don Hewett," *60 Minutes*, CBS News, 23 August 2009.

4. James A. Autry, *The Servant Leader: How to Build a Creative Team, Develop Great Morale, and Improve Bottom-Line Performance* (New York: Three Rivers Press, 2001) 20–21.

5. Thomas G. Long, *Preaching and the Literary Forms of the Bible* (Philadelphia: Fortress Press, 1989) 51.

6. Heifetz and Linsky, *Leadership on the Line,* 51-74.

7. William E. Hull, *Strategic Preaching: The Role of the Pulpit in Pastoral Leadership* (St. Louis MO: Chalice Press, 2006) 14–20.

8. Ibid., 18.

9. Cf. Martin Luther King Jr., *I Have a Dream: Writings and Speeches that Changed the World* (San Francisco: Harper, 1992).

10. Rebecca S. Chopp, *The Power to Speak: Feminism, Language, God* (New York: Crossroad, 1991) 69.

11. Annie Dillard, *Pilgrim at Tinker Creek* (New York: Harper Perennial, 1974) 33.

Chapter 6

Jesus as a Transformational Leader

As a figure in human history, Jesus prompts a multitude of reactions, many of which are evident in the New Testament Gospels. To some Jesus was a threat. To others he was a teacher. For those who followed him in faith, he became their way to know who God was and the way to what the New Testament calls "eternal life." It's important to note that eternal life didn't simply mean everlasting life. Jesus spoke not only about the "quantity" of our lives but also about the "quality" of living. To follow Jesus isn't only about our hope for a place to go after we die; it is as much about having a hope, a faith, and a love that steadies and strengthens us to live in a meaningful and caring way *right now.*

As I mentioned in an earlier chapter, one of the reasons I was deeply moved by Ronald Heifetz's term, "sacred heart," was that it describes so poignantly the essence of sincere faith. Heifetz uses terms such as "wonder, innocence, curiosity and compassion" to describe the sacred heart of the effective leader.[1] While Heifetz and I don't share precisely the same faith commitment, we do have a sacred text, the Hebrew Bible, and a desire to see leaders remain open, alive, and filled with wonder. We know how the demands of leadership affect people. Leaders can become jaded, cynical, and joyless. We start to function on "automatic pilot," but we know the intuitive people around us realize when the heart goes out of our relationships with God and with others. We find ourselves increasingly resentful, tired, and suspicious of others, and both our morale and the morale of the group suffers.

In trying to describe transformational leadership, I want to examine Jesus' life for qualities that made him such a compelling person and leader. I'm aware of the dangers of doing this. First, each of the four Gospels presents a Jesus whose claim is to be far more than an exemplary leader. While Jesus invites people to follow him, that invitation is far deeper than emulating the qualities of his leadership style.

Second, Jesus of Nazareth was not always successful in his earthly ministry. While a movement called the Christian faith blossomed from the life, death, and resurrection of Jesus, that movement didn't become robust until a number of years after his earthly death. The Gospels do not picture Jesus as the paragon of success. Jesus drew crowds to his teaching, but sometimes the demands of those same teachings caused the crowds to leave. Reading the four Gospels, especially the good news of Mark, reminds us that even Jesus' most intimate disciples often didn't understand who Jesus was and what he wanted from them. In fact, when I taught homiletics, I reminded my students that if they felt misunderstood, they should read Mark's account of Jesus' interaction with his disciples. If nothing else, these students would remember that they were in good company.

Third, I want to preface a conversation about the leadership qualities of Jesus by stating my aversion to books and articles that make Jesus a CEO or in any way portray him as a corporate business executive. Unfortunately, many people use the corporate model as a template for evaluating both churches and their ministers. What started in the first century AD as an organic, dynamic movement referred to most often as "the Way" has now become an organization functioning as a business, and the ministers are responsible for making sure the church succeeds. While nothing is inherently wrong with organization and structure, these are not the most important components of faithful living. The church is the people of God on mission to the world. Ministers are called and trained to be spiritual leaders. When these same ministers are evaluated either formally or informally by the standards of a corporate model, inevitably they experience frustration and conflict.

Identity: Being Secure with Who We Are

Most of us who have occupied positions of leadership are probably a mixture of security and insecurity. We may project an image of confidence in what we do and how we relate to people, but we know our own fears and concerns that surface in private moments.

The term "self-differentiation" describes a healthy individual.[2] A self-differentiated person knows who she is, does not need the affirmation of others to feel secure about her identity and work, and is able to focus on her work with people even if others disagree.

Of course, many of us are on a continuum between being self-differentiated and dependent. I can think of times in my ministry when I led with self-confidence. I can also recall occasions when I thought more about whether people approved of what I was doing, and my overwhelming desire to be liked blurred my sense of purpose. The more we focus on making people like us and let our identities be captured by the desire to please, the less likely others will see us as leaders. Our own dependence will draw the anger of those who see us not as people who can get things done but as people who simply want to please.

The Gospels record two pivotal qualities about Jesus' identity. *First, Jesus knew who he was.* Father Henri Nouwen writes about the baptismal experience of Jesus.[3] It's not just about the Jordan River and John the Baptizer. For Nouwen, the most profound word is when the Spirit of God descends on Jesus and the voice from heaven speaks, "This is my Son, the Beloved, with whom I am well pleased" (Matt 3:17b, NRSV).

For Nouwen, the good news is that God says this to each of us. Before Jesus did a single act of ministry, he was affirmed as the beloved child of God. Nouwen states that as followers of the Christ, this is our fundamental identity. Who we are is not based on what we do but rather on who the Creator God tells us we are. Before Jesus performs one miracle, preaches one sermon, or calls one follower, he already knows who he is—"a beloved child of God."

As New Testament scholars remind us, the four Gospels are not "real-time" accounts of the life of Jesus. The first Gospel, Mark, was probably written at least thirty years after Jesus' death. The Gospels offer the recollections of communities that gathered around their veneration of Jesus. That's one of the reasons the Gospels have discrepancies in their stories of what Jesus did and when he did it.

While the Gospels are not biographies in the strictest sense, they provide an account by these early communities of faith of what was seminal in the life of their Lord. That's why it's important that each of the four recollections contains the baptismal story. Not only did baptism mark Jesus' entrance into ministry, but it also tells us Jesus' identity, and as Henri Nouwen contends, "our identity." Beyond his family of origin, beyond whatever were the shaping events of his early years, the identity of Jesus is "God's beloved child."

The second critical component that all four Gospels address is the ability of Jesus to stay focused on his purpose. Others pressured Jesus to conform to their expectations. First-century Judaism was alive with apocalyptic anticipations of what the Messiah would be and do. Occupied and often oppressed by the Romans who ruled the land of Palestine, many Jews anticipated the Messiah to be a military and political liberator. This expectation is understandable. The Maccabean revolt had rekindled the hopes of liberation among many Jews. In their hopes, the Jews looked back to the kingship of David and remembered the monarch who went out to war.

Besides the expectations of his people, Jesus dealt with the rejection of those who felt that his ministry and message amounted to blasphemy. One of the most telling incidents for Jesus happened in his hometown of Nazareth. At the beginning of his public ministry, Jesus returned to his hometown synagogue in Nazareth. He read from the scroll of the prophet Isaiah. The message went well until he began to talk about the care of God for Gentiles like a widow in Zarepheth and a leper named Naaman the Syrian.

His listeners became incensed because this young, hometown preacher had cast the net of God's grace too far. They expected an "Anointed One" for the Jewish people. The people threatened to throw him off the cliff. In an amazing display of courage and calling,

Jesus moved through the midst of the crowd and went to the city of Capernaum, where he continued to teach (Luke 4:16-31).

Episodes like these remind us that others perceive us in different ways. They want to impose their identities on us and shape what we want to do to fit their desires, and in the process we forget our identities. Instead of seeing ourselves as beloved children of God, we perceive ourselves as unloved children who need the constant affirmation of those around us.

At the same time, Jesus, because of the awareness of who he was, listened to what other people said to him and about him. An effective leader is not someone who cuts himself off from others and forges ahead without concern about what others think or say. At Caesarea Philippi, Jesus asked his disciples two questions: "Who do others say that I am, and who do you say that I am?" The leader who prides himself on being decisive and charting a clear course without valuing the feedback of others is masking insecurity. While I may like the constant approval of others, the fact is that some of the most valuable feedback comes from people who love me enough to challenge what I do.

Jesus' identity as a loved son of the Heavenly Father gave him the certainty both to stay focused on his task and to stay connected to others. Being unconditionally loved by God gives us the power to persevere. Being loved by that same God who constantly extends the gift of love even when it means rejection gives us the freedom to be transparent and open with others.

Vision: Knowing Where We Are Going

Leaders are expected to help groups understand their reasons for existence and how best to accomplish their purposes. This is no easy task, but it's imperative for an institution, church, or any other organization to define as clearly as possible its reason for being.

Tom Long speaks cogently to the need for what he terms "the Eschatological Pulpit."[4] When I had my ordination council, I faced a divided group of ministers and laypeople. Many of them had never heard the word "eschatology," a term used by some folks to describe the "end times," but the members of the council were highly opinionated about their views of the end of history.

The council room was filled with "premillennialists." Basically, this view says the world is getting worse, and that will only change when Jesus comes a second time to establish the rule of God. The time of this rule is called the millennia, a literal thousand-year reign of Jesus on the earth. The real bone of contention among those at the ordination council wasn't about premillennialism but about the order of two events that were to accompany the millennium, "the rapture" and "the tribulation." The most divisive issue seemed to be whether the church would be "raptured," that is, taken out of this world and up to heaven, before the tribulation. The tribulation described the period of trials that would come to those on earth as Jesus came to bring God's reign. Other terms like "the War of Armageddon" were also part of this end-time mix, but by now you already get the picture of what I faced on July 22, 1965.

I had graduated from Stetson University in Deland, Florida. In my religion classes, I had heard nothing about "pre-, post-, or amillennialism." My professors rightly thought I needed to learn about more urgent topics. Fortunately, when I was in high school, a dear woman had given me a Scofield Reference Bible. Through the footnotes, I had some acquaintance with words like "millennial," "rapture," and "dispensational." But I was hardly prepared to do battle on a July night with a group of ministers who didn't even agree among themselves on these issues.

Fortunately, their lack of agreement worked to my advantage. Several days before the ordination council met, the senior minister of the church where I served met to "prep" me for the council. Since we met at his church, my minister assured me that he would be elected moderator of the council. "Here's the plan," he said. "I'll introduce you. Give a little background about yourself and tell them about your call to ministry. When the group begins to ask questions, I'll get them arguing among themselves, and you just sit there and say nothing."

The game plan worked to perfection. When somebody tried to ask me a question about whether the tribulation would precede the millennium, the moderator said something like, "Is that the way all of you see it?" Then the group began to disagree loudly while I sat like a potted plant next to my minister.

After two hours of their wrangling, I was asked to leave the room. A few minutes later, I was called into the sanctuary where I learned that I was unanimously recommended to the gospel ministry. I didn't leave that night with the best feeling. One, these ministers didn't even know me. Two, I never wanted to hear the word "eschatology" again because all it meant to me was arguing about when Jesus would come, how he would come, and where he would come. I didn't understand why all of that was so important.

Fortunately, I later came to see that this word, "eschatology," means so much more, and Tom Long has been one of my guides. He writes about it beautifully:

> First, to preach eschatologically is to participate in the promise that the fullness of God's "shalom" flows into the present, drawing it toward consummation. Eschatological preaching brings the finished work of God to bear on an unfinished world, summoning it to completion. . . . Eschatological preaching promises a "new heaven and a new earth" and invites people to participate in a coming future that, while it is not dependent upon their success, is open to the labors of their hands.[5]

Often lacking in churches when people talk about vision or vision-casting is theological undergirding. The church projects a one-year or a three-year plan (most futurists advise that the rapidity of change precludes the type of long-range planning that churches used to do), but fail to factor in the God of the present calling us to the excitement of the not yet. Churches adopt static statements of what they want to happen, but the vision remains precisely that: a series of static statements.

Reading about Jesus in the New Testament reminds us that there was a progression from life and ministry to death and resurrection. Because they wrote from a post-resurrection perspective, the Gospel writers captured this movement. Jesus operated from a vision of what it is to reveal God, and while his journey differs among the four Gospels, the destination remains the same. Yet, the vision is filled with movement, commitment, and most of all the notion that God breaks into our lives to move us toward a profound purpose. This is eschatology at its best. This isn't our trying to figure out the future of what God will do. Rather, it is being alive to the present and the future because the Divine One is alive to us and leads us into a future filled with promise.

Compassion: Caring for Others

Leadership is a unique combination of being committed to a purpose and caring for people. Some people in leadership positions are better at one part of this than the other. Task-oriented leaders like setting goals and having strategic plans. If they are more comfortable seeing their plans on paper, they may tend to communicate with others this way. The dominant form of communication is written word, usually an e-mail, where one can maintain careful records of what is said. There is much to commend this style of leadership. The task-oriented leader gets things done and has quantifiable ways to evaluate success or failure. Having goals and strategic plans are necessary for the functioning of any institution.

Other leaders are more relational. While they may spend time to develop goals and strategies, that is not their favorite way to spend a day. Usually, these leaders are more extraverted and find energy and fulfillment in interaction with other people. Organizations with this type of leadership have good morale because people feel that someone is available to listen to them. Most of us need people with whom we can share ourselves and our desires, and this type of leader is seen as a good listener who values our input. This second type of leader does not value documentation and "paper trails" as much as the task-oriented leader. She is usually found in somebody else's office, communicating information and ideas through conversations. In meetings, this leader may be less concerned about covering the ideas on the agenda and more focused on how people are feeling and doing.

While most of us have a preference for one or the other style, we need to function with a mix of the two. Problems develop when we land too heavily on one side, and needed balance is lost. Insightful leaders may surround themselves with people to help keep balance. For example, a minister who is highly task-oriented and likes to spend time in the office preparing sermons may want to have a colleague whose favorite room in the church is the fellowship hall. This type of balanced and shared leadership requires a sense of security and trust between the ministers. If I need all the attention and adulation, I will probably draw around me only those who function like me. Thus, a highly task-oriented team has no one to connect and spend time with people. On the other hand, a highly relational group makes some people wonder if anything ever gets done. Some people want to know clearly, "What is our vision, and how are we going to achieve it?" Everything else is interpreted as "small talk."

When we look at Jesus, we find a unique combination of someone who knew what he was about and at the same time related to people. In Matthew's Gospel, many of the teachings of Jesus are pulled together in what we call the "Sermon on the Mount." Interestingly, this is not a long sermon. When read aloud with the appropriate pauses, the sermon takes 12–15 minutes. In Matthew 5–7, Jesus lays out the moral and ethical implications of his message, and he also creates a challenging vision for the disciples. Jesus instructs his followers that they are like "salt" and "light" to the world. That is the metaphorical identity of the disciples. Then Jesus calls them to live out their identities in the world.

At the end of the same Gospel, Jesus speaks what we term now as the "Great Commission." The followers of Jesus are given a vision of the world. Undoubtedly, the Matthean community for whom these words were vital could have opted for something less bold given their circumstances. Written after the destruction of the Jewish temple by the Romans and trying to find footing as a distinct faith and not just a sect of Judaism, the Christian community could have chosen a vision that was more about existence rather than extension. Yet, Matthew has the risen Christ calling a struggling band of believers, "Go therefore and make disciples of all nations, baptizing them in the name of the Father, and of the Son, and of the Holy Spirit, and teaching them to obey everything that I have commanded you" (Matt 28:19-20a).

This is no vision for the timid. Yet, what is remarkable is the way Jesus weaves his compassionate presence into this call to commitment. Jesus prefaces the Great Commission by telling these disciples, "All authority in heaven and on earth has been given to me" (28:18b). Maybe even more remarkable is the final promise that concludes Matthew's Gospel: ". . . and remember I am with you always, to the end of the age" (28:20b).

Jesus is a leader for whom task and relationship are closely aligned. Instead of separating vision from the personal promise of his presence, Jesus brings the two together. People need to have both direction and the promise of the leader's care and compassion. The challenge for anybody who wants to lead is to recognize where his strength lies and then work to build the other dimensions of leadership.

In fact, if Jesus is the model of transformational leadership, he gives us no choice about being either task-oriented or people-oriented. It's not either-or but both-and. Writing about the preaching event, Stanley Hauerwas offers a profound word that applies to both proclamation and leadership: "The presumption that the gospel is 'all about us' too often leads us to think that 'good' sermons are those 'I got something out of.' But sermons, at least if they are faithful to Scripture, are not about us—they are about God."[6]

Just as the preacher who is obsessed with preaching "good" sermons that connect with listeners can become self-centered wondering if people will be receptive, so leaders can become inadvertently self-centered if pleasing people trumps purpose or if achieving the purpose makes us insensitive to people's needs. Again, it's not either-or but both-and.

We need to be cautious when we talk about sensitivity to people. That doesn't mean pleasing everybody, which is impossible. We often deal with people who have their own agendas or who will never be pleased with much of what we try to do. We listen and care the best we can, but compassion sometimes involves confrontation. A careful reading of Jesus' ministry reminds us that compassion is caring, but sometimes it's caring enough to confront.

Risk: Being Willing to Fail

In her excellent book, *The Practicing Congregation*, Diana Butler Bass draws on the insights of Urban Holmes when she speaks about the need for imagination in the life of the church: "Urban Holmes suggested that imagination is an act of pilgrimage—of going 'outside the city' to find God's presence. 'The city' may be the accepted way of doing things, listening to the approved narrative, following the proven program."[7]

One of the things Jesus "imagined" and taught was a new kind of world in which people treated each other as they wanted to be treated. Jesus' ministered with a vision that included the dispossessed, the marginalized, and those often overlooked by others. Continuing in the tradition of Hebrew prophets like Micah, Jesus reiterated the message, "He has told you, O Mortal, what is good; and what does the LORD require of you but to do justice, and to love kindness, and to walk humbly with your God?" (Mic 6:8).

In the Sermon on the Mount, Jesus called his disciples to a radical way of life. Both attitudes and actions were important. While you and I might not murder someone, Jesus called us to assess whether we hold festering resentment or jealousy that may keep us from being fully open and alive to others. Even in our praying, Jesus warned against empty phrases designed to please others. Prayer may consist of few words, but we speak those to God with an open spirit.

Like many leaders, Jesus was counter-cultural. He called people to profound change, and, of course, change is never easy. While Jesus had followers, he also had powerful enemies. Finally, Jesus lost the earthly battle, and for those of us who are his followers, the cross is a continuing symbol of what can happen if the voice of change is perceived as insurrection and then silenced.

Few of us set out to fail. Maybe some people don't believe they deserve success, but most of us who try to lead want to succeed. However, even the best leaders succeed only some of the time. The fear of failure may so inhibit what we do that ultimately we settle for a management style that does little more than perpetuate the institutional status quo. What we do is designed to please those around us, and if there is a need to change, courageous voices are intimidated or silenced.

This is hardly an excuse to come into a group with our own agenda and with no sensitivity to the patterns of an organization or to the people in the group. As I've said before, change is always perceived as loss, and loss provokes grief and anger. If we try to change something, we need to introduce the change incrementally and be willing to back off if the change is too threatening. If we are the kinds of people who want change to happen by sunrise tomorrow, we probably will spend much of our lives discouraged and frustrated.

As I write this, the United States is embroiled in a heated discourse about a national health policy. As vital as this is, the issue itself has become caught up in what some people see as "uncivil discourse." A decade ago, Deborah Tannen wrote about the "argument culture" in the United States.[8] Tannen, a well-respected linguist from Georgetown University, expressed deep concern about a growing "aggression" in the rhetoric of the media and in the public forum. What Tannen wrote about has only accelerated in the last decade. Rhetoric that appeals to emotions demonizes people but doesn't truly discuss the issues. Some of this aggressive speech finds its way into the church house, and the mission of the church is lost in the heat of personal accusations that only engender more heat and less light.

Frankly, Jesus became angry on occasion during his ministry. It's hard to imagine his turning over the money-changers' tables in the temple with a smile on his face. Yet, much more often he showed respect and care for people. Ministers today who like to turn over tables and act out their frustrations are likely to create an environment that rarely experiences change.

What marks Jesus' ministry is his focus on what God called him to do and his sense of purpose in moving toward that vision. Jesus experienced success and failure, acceptance and rejection. However, he never paused too long to accept accolades or pulled inside himself in a ball of pity when he wasn't warmly received. He moved on regardless of the responses. Jesus had a mission. Success and failure were not his evaluative scales. Faithfulness was. In a society where people are too quickly identified as winners and losers by how well they do, Jesus displays faithfulness to God that undergirds us in the journey.

Communication: Speaking What Matters

Much of what we know about Jesus comes from the reflections of the early communities of faith about who Jesus was and what he believed was critical. The Pauline corpus of writings, while written prior to the four Gospels, reflects the development of the early churches, how they were organized, and some of the theological and moral problems they faced.

The Gospels, written probably thirty to sixty years following the death of Jesus, make no pretense about being a word-for-word account of Jesus' life and teaching, but they are a rich reservoir of inspiration that allow us to look through the eyes of his followers at the Jesus whom they served. In looking through these communities' eyes at what Jesus preached and taught, we find several components of the substance and style of Jesus' communication.

First, Jesus saw himself as *part of the great story of God at work in the world*. Jesus didn't suddenly appear on the stage of history without divine background. He was part of the tradition of the First Testament of Scripture. His bible was the bible of his forebears. Jesus was not some spiritual sideshow or even the intentional founder of a new religion. During his ministry, Jesus challenged some of the interpretations of the Torah, but at no point did he disown his heritage. Jesus' followers were known as "Messianists" because they saw him as the fulfillment of Jewish hopes for a "messiah" or "anointed one." A separation developed only after the fall of the temple in Jerusalem in AD 70 and the attendant tensions between Orthodox Judaism and the Messianists.

What does this have to do with communication? Good rhetoricians see themselves as part of the human story and as part of the story of the people to whom they speak. This doesn't mean our speeches are simply chronicles of the past, but they are informed by the remembrance and the collective memory of people.

For example, a minister needs to remember that she is part of the great story of God. She speaks with the authority not only of one who appears on the scene for a moment in time but who in some mysterious way is part of the whole story of God who has been at work, is at work, and will be at work. What we say is not only about us and our novel twist on a biblical text. We don't walk to the podium as if we are the only ones who have ever tried to give voice to what matters.

To see ourselves as isolated individuals who must make God interesting is a fearful task. It can also drive us to think about ways to keep the audience interested in a message we've already decided is intrinsically dull. Any speaker who speaks words that make a difference has to believe those words can make a difference. We must believe in the power of the message. Otherwise, our talk becomes filled with small talk, unconnected anecdotes, and bland stories that begin with, "A funny thing happened to me on the way to church today!"

This isn't a call for us to be overly serious in speaking the message. Humor is a powerful communicative tool. But the best humor is not jokes we read on the Internet or hear at some conference. Most speakers are guilty of forcing a seemingly good story into our message only to watch it die because it didn't fit.

A second ingredient in Jesus' preaching was his *freshness*. As I've mentioned, Matthew records at the end of the Sermon on the Mount that the crowds who overheard Jesus' words were "astounded" at his teachings, "for he taught them as one having authority, and not as their scribes" (Matt 7:29).

Some of us shy away from the word "authority" because it carries negative connotations that we resist. For those of us who are more moderate or mainstream in our theological views, authority may connote the kind of preacher who brooks no disagreement and gives the impression that everything he says should be accepted with no dissent. In response, some ministers move to the other side and become almost apologetic about anything they say. Openness and insecurity are not synonyms. Many people today look for some sound of certainty in their lives. When we speak and mumble, dipping our heads without any eye contact, and intersperse our sermons with phrases like, "I think" or "I'm not sure," and then apologize for taking up people's time, the impression is that what we say doesn't make much difference to us.

The freshness of Jesus' message was that the messenger internalized it. He wasn't delivering a speech. He was delivering himself, the things that were essential to his life, and the ideas that shaped the fabric of his being. Most of all, Jesus reflected both in his being and in his doing the God who gave ultimate meaning to life. Jesus wasn't taking time from people with many more things to do with their time. Rather, he spoke with the urgency and conviction of someone who gave meaning to the times of our lives.

A leader who speaks to a group wants to articulate a vision clearly but also to inspire and motivate people to dream dreams and to act on those dreams. Will everybody who listens to us agree with us or connect to the passion we feel? Of course not! Over a period of time, that lack of positive response may curb the enthusiasm of the leader until our talking becomes little more than "Here we go again."

For ministers, this is always a vocational hazard. We receive negative criticism and, perhaps worse, little or no reaction from our congregation. After a while, some ministers become worn down because they conclude that their efforts are fruitless. We need to remember that the test of preaching is never "audience analysis" or "Did they respond to what I said?" It's wonderful that some people who heard Jesus deliver the Sermon on the Mount thought he spoke with authority. However, consider the vast numbers who left the mountain that day and said nothing about what Jesus did. What motivates us is not that everybody concludes that we're great speakers with the gift of words, but that we are committed to a message that has changed us and can change others. However, we are not responsible for the hearing and certainly not for the changing of others. "Some seed falls on rocky ground," Jesus stated in a parable (Mark 4:1-8). As leaders, we work to state the vision clearly, and we call people to transforming change. What happens is then in God's hands.

L. Gregory Jones, former Dean of the Divinity School at Duke University, tells about the encounter of an Old Testament professor with a student.[9] Dissatisfied with his grade on an exegesis paper, the student asked how he could improve his grade. "Become a deeper person," the professor replied. That is the goal of transformation. We do better because we are becoming better, deeper persons. Much needs to be done in our world. Will the deep, transformational leader please stand up?

Notes

1. Ronald A. Heifetz and Marty Linsky, *Leadership on the Line: Staying Alive through the Dangers of Leading* (Boston: Harvard Business School, 2002) 225–36.

2. Peter L. Steinke, *Healthy Congregations: A Systems Approach* (New York: Alban Institute Publication, 1996) 96.

3. Henri Nouwen, *Life of the Beloved: Spiritual Living in a Secular World* (New York: Crossroad, 1992) 25–33.

4. Thomas G. Long, *Preaching from Memory to Hope* (Louisville: John Knox Press, 2009) 125.

5. Ibid.

6. Stanley Hauerwas, *A Cross-Shattered Church: Reclaiming the Theological Heart of Preaching* (Grand Rapids MI: Brazos Press, 2009) 14–15.

7. Diana Butler Bass, *The Practicing Congregation: Imagining a New Old Church* (Herndon VA: Alban Institute, 2004) 94.

8. Deborah Tannen, *The Argument Culture: Stopping America's War of Words* (New York: Ballantine Books, 1998).

9. L. Gregory Jones, "Embodying Scripture in the Community of Faith," *The Art of Reading Scripture*, ed. Ellen F. Davis and Richard B. Hays (Grand Rapids MI: William B. Eerdmans Publishing Co., 2003) 156.

Afterword

Woven through all of Paul's letters is one admonition: "Become *more* of who you already are!" Chuck Bugg grasps this idea and shares it with his particular skill in these pages. Transformational leadership is a difficult concept to grasp, much less unpack. However, from the beginning of this book, Chuck does so with a masterful combination of transparent personal stories and inspired intellectual insights. He models for us approaches he tries to convey.

I have been blessed to be colleague, friend, and ministry partner with Chuck. I know firsthand how he continues to practice the ideas he puts forward in this writing. He constantly seeks to become *more* of who he already is. His interactions with Ron Heifetz challenged Chuck and led in part to this book. As we "eavesdrop" on their conversations, we are further challenged, inspired, and blessed.

Leadership is a combination of art and science. Leaders are not "born" into leadership. Effective leaders constantly study themselves and examine their skills in order to become more effective. Effective leaders have to navigate the challenges of authority, power, ego, and personal change. Effective leaders change from "the inside out" and then begin witnessing change from the "outside in." Chuck takes the time to walk us through each of these thoughts, unpack them for us, and reveal a bit of himself in the process. We as readers are blessed and challenged in the process.

Transformational leadership is the embodiment of a combination of factors. Transformational leaders work from a stance of establishing trust, engaging with passion, living with humility, and leading coherently. These are not easy to internalize! But the challenge to become *more* of who we already are leads us to continue in the process. We continue to become better, and we find ourselves doing better. This is not a magical formula but the result of self-study, practice, and the grace of those around us.

Chuck Bugg is one of my heroes! I'm grateful for the challenges he continues to put before us. He is not content to rest on his laurels. He is not content for us to do so, either. About midway through chapter 1, he sums up the entire book for me when he says, "Ministers must change!" Chuck knows that the church is in need of transformation and transformational leaders. He doesn't simply tell us "what"; he attempts to tell us "how"!

Chuck has challenged us to become *more* of who we already are. Even as he challenges us, he challenges himself. This represents the best of his book for me. Chuck is engaged with us in this journey. He is a practitioner and a thinker. He is a teacher and a student. He is a minister and a pilgrim. He is a transformational leader and a transformational follower. Above everything else, he is my friend, and his friendship challenges each of us to become even more of who we already are.

Bo Prosser
Coordinator for Congregational Formation
Cooperative Baptist Fellowship
Atlanta, Georgia

Other available titles from

#Connect
Reaching Youth Across the Digital Divide
Brian Foreman

Reaching our youth across the digital divide is a struggle for parents, ministers, and other adults who work with Generation Z— today's teenagers. *#Connect* leads readers into the technological landscape, encourages conversations with teenagers, and reminds us all to be the presence of Christ in every facet of our lives. *978-1-57312-693-9 120 pages/pb $13.00*

Beginnings
A Reverend and a Rabbi Talk About the Stories of Genesis
Michael Smith and Rami Shapiro

Editor Aaron Herschel Shapiro describes storytelling as an "infinite game" because stories "must be retold—not just repeated, but reinvented, reimagined, and reexperienced" to remain vital in the world. Mike and Rami continue their conversations from the *Mount and Mountain* books, exploring the places where their traditions intersect and diverge, listening to each other as they respond to the stories of creation, of Adam and Eve, Cain and Abel, Noah, Jacob, and Joseph. *978-1-57312-772-1 202 pages/pb $18.00*

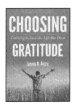

Choosing Gratitude
Learning to Love the Life You Have
James A. Autry

Autry reminds us that gratitude is a choice, a spiritual—not social—process. He suggests that if we cultivate gratitude as a way of being, we may not change the world and its ills, but we can change our response to the world. If we fill our lives with moments of gratitude, we will indeed love the life we have. *978-1-57312-614-4 144 pages/pb $15.00*

Choosing Gratitude 365 Days a Year
Your Daily Guide to Grateful Living
James A. Autry and Sally J. Pederson

Filled with quotes, poems, and the inspired voices of both Pederson and Autry, in a society consumed by fears of not having "enough"— money, possessions, security, and so on—this book suggests that if we cultivate gratitude as a way of being, we may not change the world and its ills, but we can change our response to the world. *978-1-57312-689-2 210 pages/pb $18.00*

To order call 1-800-747-3016 or visit www.helwys.com

Contextualizing the Gospel
A Homiletic Commentary on 1 Corinthians

Brian L. Harbour

Harbour examines every part of Paul's letter, providing a rich resource for those who want to struggle with the difficult texts as well as the simple texts, who want to know how God's word—all of it—intersects with their lives today. 978-1-57312-589-5 240 pages/pb **$19.00**

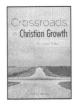

Crossroads in Christian Growth
W. Loyd Allen

Authentic Christian life presents spiritual crises and we struggle to find a hero walking with God at a crossroads. With wisdom and sincerity, W. Loyd Allen presents Jesus as our example and these crises as stages in the journey of growth we each take toward maturity in Christ. 978-1-57312-753-0 164 pages/pb **$15.00**

A Divine Duet
Ministry and Motherhood

Alicia Davis Porterfield, ed.

Each essay in this inspiring collection is as different as the mother-minister who wrote it, from theologians to chaplains, inner-city ministers to rural-poverty ministers, youth pastors to preachers, mothers who have adopted, birthed, and done both. 978-1-57312-676-2 146 pages/pb **$16.00**

Ethics as if Jesus Mattered
Essays in Honor of Glen H. Stassen

Rick Axtell, Michelle Tooley, Michael L. Westmoreland-White, eds.

Ethics as if Jesus Mattered will introduce Stassen's work to a new generation, advance dialogue and debate in Christian ethics, and inspire more faithful discipleship just as it honors one whom the contributors consider a mentor. 978-1-57312-695-3 234 pages/pb **$18.00**

Ezekiel (Smyth & Helwys Annual Bible Study series)
God's Presence in Performance

William D. Shiell

Through a four-session Bible study for individuals and groups, Shiell interprets the book of Ezekiel as a four-act drama to be told to adult, children, and youth groups living out their faith in a strange, new place. The book encourages congregations to listen to God's call, accept where God has planted them, surrender the shame of their past, receive a new heart from God, and allow God to breathe new life into them.

Teaching Guide 978-1-57312-755-4 192 pages/pb **$14.00**
Study Guide 978-1-57312-756-1 126 pages/pb **$6.00**

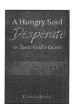

A Hungry Soul Desperate to Taste God's Grace
Honest Prayers for Life
Charles Qualls

Part of how we *see* God is determined by how we *listen* to God. There is so much noise and movement in the world that competes with images of God. This noise would drown out God's beckoning voice and distract us. Charles Qualls's newest book offers readers prayers for that journey toward the meaning and mystery of God.   *978-1-57312-648-9 152 pages/pb* **$14.00**

If Jesus Isn't the Answer . . . He Sure Asks the Right Questions!
J. Daniel Day

Taking eleven of Jesus' questions as its core, Day invites readers into their own conversation with Jesus. Equal parts testimony, theological instruction, pastoral counseling, and autobiography, the book is ultimately an invitation to honest Christian discipleship.

978-1-57312-797-4 148 pages/pb **$16.00**

I'm Trying to Lead . . . Is Anybody Following?
The Challenge of Congregational Leadership in the Postmodern World
Charles B. Bugg

Bugg provides us with a view of leadership that has theological integrity, honors the diversity of church members, and reinforces the brave hearts of church leaders who offer vision and take risks in the service of Christ and the church.   *978-1-57312-731-8 136 pages/pb* **$13.00**

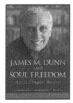

James M. Dunn and Soul Freedom
Aaron Douglas Weaver

James Milton Dunn, over the last fifty years, has been the most aggressive Baptist proponent for religious liberty in the United States. Soul freedom—voluntary, uncoerced faith and an unfettered individual conscience before God—is the basis of his understanding of church-state separation and the historic Baptist basis of religious liberty.   *978-1-57312-590-1 224 pages/pb* **$18.00**

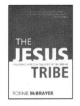

The Jesus Tribe
Following Christ in the Land of the Empire
Ronnie McBrayer

The Jesus Tribe fleshes out the implications, possibilities, contradictions, and complexities of what it means to live within the Jesus Tribe and in the shadow of the American Empire.

978-1-57312-592-5 208 pages/pb **$17.00**

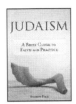

Judaism
A Brief Guide to Faith and Practice
Sharon Pace

Sharon Pace's newest book is a sensitive and comprehensive introduction to Judaism. What is it like to be born into the Jewish community? How does belief in the One God and a universal morality shape the way in which Jews see the world? How does one find meaning in life and the courage to endure suffering? How does one mark joy and forge community ties? *978-1-57312-644-1 144 pages/pb* **$16.00**

Living Call
An Old Church and a Young Minister Find Life Together
Tony Lankford

This light look at church and ministry highlights the dire need for fidelity to the vocation of church leadership. It also illustrates Lankford's conviction that the historic, local congregation has a beautiful, vibrant, and hopeful future. *978-1-57312-702-8 112 pages/pb* **$12.00**

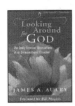

Looking Around for God
The Strangely Reverent Observations of an Unconventional Christian
James A. Autry

Looking Around for God, Autry's tenth book, is in many ways his most personal. In it he considers his unique life of faith and belief in God. Autry is a former Fortune 500 executive, author, poet, and consultant whose work has had a significant influence on leadership thinking.
978-157312-484-3 144 pages/pb **$16.00**

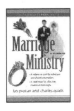

Marriage Ministry: A Guidebook
Bo Prosser and Charles Qualls

This book is equally helpful for ministers, for nearly/newlywed couples, and for thousands of couples across our land looking for fresh air in their marriages. *1-57312-432-X 160 pages/pb* **$16.00**

Meeting Jesus Today
For the Cautious, the Curious, and the Committed
Jeanie Miley

Meeting Jesus Today, ideal for both individual study and small groups, is intended to be used as a workbook. It is designed to move readers from studying the Scriptures and ideas within the chapters to recording their journey with the Living Christ.
978-1-57312-677-9 320 pages/pb **$19.00**

The Ministry Life
101 Tips for Ministers' Spouses
John and Anne Killinger

While no pastor does his or her work alone, roles for a spouse or partner are much more flexible and fluid in the twenty-first century than they once were. Spouses who want to support their minister-mates' vocation may wonder where to begin. The Killingers' suggestions are notable for their range of interests; whatever your talents may be, the Killingers have identified a way to put those gifts to work in tasks both large and small.

978-1-57312-769-1 252 pages/pb **$19.00**

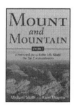

The Ministry Life
101 Tips for New Ministers
John Killinger

Sharing years of wisdom from more than fifty years in ministry and teaching, *The Ministry Life: 101 Tips for New Ministers* by John Killinger is filled with practical advice and wisdom for a minister's day-to-day tasks as well as advice on intellectual and spiritual habits to keep ministers of any age healthy and fulfilled.

978-1-57312-662-5 244 pages/pb **$19.00**

Mount and Mountain
Vol. 1: A Reverend and a Rabbi Talk About the Ten Commandments
Rami Shapiro and Michael Smith

Mount and Mountain represents the first half of an interfaith dialogue—a dialogue that neither preaches nor placates but challenges its participants to work both singly and together in the task of reinterpreting sacred texts. Mike and Rami discuss the nature of divinity, the power of faith, the beauty of myth and story, the necessity of doubt, the achievements, failings, and future of religion, and, above all, the struggle to live ethically and in harmony with the way of God.

978-1-57312-612-0 144 pages/pb **$15.00**

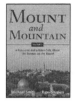

Mount and Mountain
Vol. 2: A Reverend and a Rabbi Talk About the Sermon on the Mount
Rami Shapiro and Michael Smith

This book, focused on the Sermon on the Mount, represents the second half of Mike and Rami's dialogue. In it, Mike and Rami explore the text of Jesus' sermon cooperatively, contributing perspectives drawn from their lives and religious traditions and seeking moments of illumination.

978-1-57312-654-0 254 pages/pb **$19.00**

Of Mice and Ministers
Musings and Conversations About Life, Death, Grace, and Everything

Bert Montgomery

With stories about pains, joys, and everyday life, *Of Mice and Ministers* finds Jesus in some unlikely places and challenges us to do the same. From tattooed women ministers to saying the "N"-word to the brotherly kiss, Bert Montgomery takes seriously the lesson from Psalm 139—where can one go that God is not already there?   *978-1-57312-733-2 154 pages/pb* **$14.00**

Overcoming Adolescence
Growing Beyond Childhood into Maturity

Marion D. Aldridge

In *Overcoming Adolescence*, Marion D. Aldridge poses questions for adults of all ages to consider. His challenge to readers is one he has personally worked to confront: to grow up *all the way*—mentally, physically, academically, socially, emotionally, and spiritually. The key involves not only knowing how to work through the process but also how to recognize what may be contributing to our perpetual adolescence.

978-1-57312-577-2 156 pages/pb **$17.00**

Preacher Breath
Sermon & Essays

Kyndall Rae Rothaus

"The task of preaching is such an oddly wonderful, strangely beautiful experience. . . . Kyndall Rothaus's *Preacher Breath* is a worthy guide, leading the reader room by room with wisdom, depth, and a spiritual maturity far beyond her years, so that the preaching house becomes a holy, joyful home. . . . This book is soul kindle for a preacher's heart."

—Danielle Shroyer
Pastor and Author of *The Boundary-Breaking God*
978-1-57312-734-9 208 pages/pb **$16.00**

Quiet Faith
An Introvert's Guide to Spiritual Survival

Judson Edwards

In eight finely crafted chapters, Edwards looks at key issues like evangelism, interpreting the Bible, dealing with doubt, and surviving the church from the perspective of a confirmed, but sometimes reluctant, introvert. In the process, he offers some provocative insights that introverts will find helpful and reassuring.   *978-1-57312-681-6 144 pages/pb* **$15.00**

Reading Deuteronomy
(Reading the Old Testament series)
A Literary and Theological Commentary
Stephen L. Cook

A lost treasure for large segments of the modern world, the book of Deuteronomy powerfully repays contemporary readers' attention. God's presence and Word in Deuteronomy stir deep longing for God and move readers to a place of intimacy with divine otherness, holism, and will for person-centered community. The consistently theological interpretation reveals the centrality of Deuteronomy for faith and counters critical accusations about violence, intolerance, and polytheism in the book.　*978-1-57312-757-8 286 pages/pb* **$22.00**

Reading Hosea–Micah
(Reading the Old Testament series)
A Literary and Theological Commentary
Terence E. Fretheim

Terence E. Fretheim explores themes of indictment, judgment, and salvation in Hosea–Micah. The indictment against the people of God especially involves issues of idolatry, as well as abuse of the poor and needy. The effects of such behaviors are often horrendous in their severity. While God is often the subject of such judgments, the consequences, like fruit, grow out of the deed itself.　*978-1-57312-687-8 224 pages/pb* **$22.00**

Reflective Faith
A Theological Toolbox for Women
Tony W. Cartledge

In *Reflective Faith*, Susan Shaw offers a set of tools to explore difficult issues of biblical interpretation, theology, church history, and ethics—especially as they relate to women. Reflective faith invites intellectual struggle and embraces the unknown; it is a way of discipleship, a way to love God with your mind, as well as your heart, your soul, and your strength.

978-1-57312-719-6 292 pages/pb **$24.00**

Workbook *978-1-57312-754-7 164 pages/pb* **$12.00**

Sessions with Psalms (Session Bible Studies series)
Prayers for All Seasons
Eric and Alicia D. Porterfield

Sessions with Psalms is a ten-session study unit designed to explore what it looks like for the words of the psalms to become the words of our prayers. Each session is followed by a thought-provoking page of questions that allow for a deeper experience of the scriptural passages. These resource pages can be used by seminar leaders during preparation and group discussion, as well as in individual Bible study.　*978-1-57312-768-4 136 pages/pb* **$14.00**

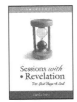

Sessions with Revelation (Session Bible Studies series)
The Final Days of Evil
David Sapp

David Sapp's careful guide through Revelation demonstrates that it is a letter of hope for believers; it is less about the last days of history than it is about the last days of evil. Without eliminating its mystery, Sapp unlocks Revelation's central truths so that its relevance becomes clear. *978-1-57312-706-6 166 pages/pb* **$14.00**

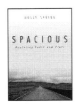

Spacious
Exploring Faith and Place
Holly Sprink

Exploring where we are and why that matters to God is an ongoing process. If we are present and attentive, God creatively and continuously widens our view of the world. *978-1-57312-649-6 156 pages/pb* **$16.00**

The Teaching Church
Congregation as Mentor
Christopher M. Hamlin / Sarah Jackson Shelton

Collected in *The Teaching Church: Congregation as Mentor* are the stories of the pastors who shared how congregations have shaped, nurtured, and, sometimes, broken their resolve to be faithful servants of God. *978-1-57312-682-3 112 pages/pb* **$13.00**

Time for Supper
Invitations to Christ's Table
Brett Younger

Some scholars suggest that every meal in literature is a communion scene. Could every meal in the Bible be a communion text? Could every passage be an invitation to God's grace? At the Lord's Table we experience sorrow, hope, friendship, and forgiveness. These meditations on the Lord's Supper help us listen to the myriad of ways God invites us to gratefully, reverently, and joyfully share the cup of Christ. *978-1-57312-720-2 246 pages/pb* **$18.00**

A Time to Laugh
Humor in the Bible

Mark E. Biddle

An extension of his well-loved seminary course on humor in the Bible, *A Time to Laugh* draws on Mark E. Biddle's command of Hebrew language and cultural subtleties to explore the ways humor was intentionally incorporated into Scripture. With characteristic liveliness, Biddle guides the reader through the stories of six biblical characters who did rather unexpected things.   *978-1-57312-683-0 164 pages/pb* **$14.00**

The World Is Waiting for You
Celebrating the 50th Ordination Anniversary of Addie Davis

Pamela R. Durso & LeAnn Gunter Johns, eds.

Hope for the church and the world is alive and well in the words of these gifted women. Keen insight, delightful observations, profound courage, and a gift for communicating the good news are woven throughout these sermons. The Spirit so evident in Addie's calling clearly continues in her legacy.   *978-1-57312-732-5 224 pages/pb* **$18.00**

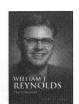

William J. Reynolds
Church Musician

David W. Music

William J. Reynolds is renowned among Baptist musicians, music ministers, song leaders, and hymnody students. In eminently readable style, David W. Music's comprehensive biography describes Reynolds's family and educational background, his career as a minister of music, denominational leader, and seminary professor.   *978-1-57312-690-8 358 pages/pb* **$23.00**

With Us in the Wilderness
Finding God's Story in Our Lives

Laura A. Barclay

What stories compose your spiritual biography? In *With Us in the Wilderness*, Laura Barclay shares her own stories of the intersection of the divine and the everyday, guiding readers toward identifying and embracing God's presence in their own narratives.

978-1-57312-721-9 120 pages/pb **$13.00**

Made in the USA
Columbia, SC
08 September 2021

44949767R00067